John Walter Cross

Impressions of Dante and of the New World

John Walter Cross

Impressions of Dante and of the New World

ISBN/EAN: 9783744713344

Printed in Europe, USA, Canada, Australia, Japan

Cover: Foto ©Thomas Meinert / pixelio.de

More available books at **www.hansebooks.com**

IMPRESSIONS OF DANTE

AND OF

THE NEW WORLD

WITH A FEW WORDS ON BIMETALLISM

BY

J. W. CROSS

WILLIAM BLACKWOOD AND SONS
EDINBURGH AND LONDON
MDCCCXCIII

PREFACE.

"Don't shoot the organist; he's doing his level best." This ancient American story of a notice prominently affixed in a church in the Wild West, as a gentle appeal to the congregation, expresses the mildly deprecatory attitude that I desire to assume to my readers—if I have any—or rather the attitude that I hope they will assume to me. "Don't shoot the essayist; he's doing his level best." I confess that it is difficult to find a valid excuse for republishing old magazine articles, and in my own case I cannot plead that any host of admiring friends has put pressure on me to collect mine. I take it that the real reason for these republications is always the same—a desire on the part of the writer to leave some print of his footsteps, however shallow, on the sands of time. It must be admitted that this reason is not a very urgent one for readers, and may even prove to be slightly pathetic for the writer if it happens that no copies of his book are sold. One copy must always go to the British Museum, and that is a record of his existence on this troublous planet. But it is rather like a tombstone record. For I protest that, with the exception of one's feelings in a cemetery, I know scarcely any sensation more depressing than to stand on the floor of the great reading-room in Bloomsbury and let the eye follow, till the head is dizzy, the huge circles of books, hundreds of thousands of which no eye but the author's has ever looked at. What a grave of reputations! What a mute appeal to our sympathies in the long labour, the hopes and fears, the joys and sorrows that went to the making of all these unread, and mostly unnecessary, volumes! Fortunately mine is "only a little one." I hope that the first three essays may have some general interest. Perhaps this may prove to be a harmless delusion on my part, and hope's flattering tale may be rudely contradicted by Messrs Blackwoods' account of sales. If the first three have no general interest, I expect that the remainder will generally be looked on as rather ancient history. But history has its uses—even though it be true that it never repeats itself. And there is a certain interest (especially, let us admit, to the author!) in noting the progress of the matters reviewed in twenty years, and in learning from later events whether any of the results were more or less clearly deducible from the premisses. The state of things in the United States during the suspension of specie payments and after resumption, must always arrest the attention of business men, economists, and currency doctors. In any time, too, of great commercial depression, it is good to know that another country has been through the same mill before, and has come out safely. I doubt if the financial condition of any country was ever more depressed than that of the United States in 1877. The year lives in my memory as characterised by the shrewdly humorous remark of an American to an English fellow-traveller on a Cunard steamer. "The fact is, sir, that trade is so powerful bad in my country, that although I am now on my honeymoon trip to Europe, I really couldn't afford to bring my wife along!" Events have since proved that *time* is all that is wanted in a new, rich, and undeveloped country with an energetic and mainly honest population. The three forces that have enabled the United States to pull through their troubles so quickly and so successfully are—immigration, the extension of railroads, and the assurance of peace. There is no blood-tax, and consequently all the energies of the entire population are devoted to the production of useful and agreeable things possessing exchangeable value—or in other words, to the production of wealth. And if the question be asked, What connection has Dante with the New World? I am inclined to answer it in his own words from the 'De Monarchiâ.' "It has thus been sufficiently set forth that the proper work of the human race, taken as a whole, is to set in action the whole capacity of that understanding which is capable of development: first in the way of speculation, and then by its extension in the way of action. And seeing that what is true of a part is true also of the whole, and that it is by *rest and quiet* that the individual man becomes perfect in wisdom and prudence; so the human race, *by living in the calm and tranquillity of peace*, applies itself most freely and easily to its proper work—a work which, according to the saying, 'Thou hast made him a little lower than the angels,' is almost divine. And hence the word which sounded to the shepherds from above was not riches, nor pleasure, nor honour, nor length of life, nor health, nor strength, nor beauty; but *peace*. For the heavenly host said, 'Glory to God in the highest, and on earth peace to men of goodwill.' Therefore also '*Peace be with you*' was the salutation of the Saviour of mankind. For it behoved Him, who was the greatest of Saviours, to utter in His greeting the greatest of saving blessings." Three hundred years, too, after Dante's death, Bacon, in his 'Novum Organon,' remarks with the prophetic vision of true genius, "the breath of hope blows on us from that Continent." What is this breath of hope which has now become a pervading atmosphere over half the planet? It is the freedom from the continual dread of war. The New World rests on the basis of industrialism as opposed to militarism. In this single nineteenth century we have seen a nation, which has had the good fortune to be able to establish itself on this basis, grow to be 65 millions of people holding one of the most commanding positions in the world. If it can maintain that position without further war, the example must have a beneficent effect on Europe; for although the circumstances of the two hemispheres are so widely different, success will always have its admirers and its great influence. Every day saved from war is a day gained, and the union in sentiment of all the English-speaking peoples —nearly 120 million of them to-day—will always be the strongest guarantee of peace.

In conclusion, I must apologise for the defects of style in these papers. They are not put forward as literature but as impressions—and as impressions they must be judged. Let me not forget, too, the chief *raison d'être* of a preface to reprints—namely, to thank the proprietors of the various magazines—'Blackwood's,' 'Nineteenth Century,' 'Fraser's,' 'Macmillan's,' and the 'Contemporary'—for their courtesy in permitting the republication.

J. W. C.

QUEEN ANNE'S MANSIONS,
October 1892.

CONTENTS.

	PAGE
DANTE FOR THE GENERAL,	1
DANTE AND THE "NEW REFORMATION,"	66
THE NEW WORLD,	110
ON THE EXTENSION OF RAILWAYS IN AMERICA,	134
THE FUTURE OF THE AGRICULTURAL LABOURERS' EMIGRATION,	163
AMERICA REDIVIVA,	199
THE FUTURE OF FOOD,	236
SOCIAL NEW YORK,	266
CONCLUSION: WITH A FEW WORDS ON BIMETALLISM,	294

ESSAYS.

DANTE FOR THE GENERAL.[1]

A WORD of apology, or at any rate of explanation, seems almost to be required from any one who, without special qualification, writes about Dante at this period of the world's history. The excuse and the motive are in effect one. Within the last few years Dante may be said to have become popular—popular in the widest use of the term—both in England and in America. A new generation of readers, drawn in many cases from fresh social strata, approach a poet (and particularly a poet whose writing is in a sense sacred) in a different attitude from that of the select few to whom the poems have hitherto been a special cult:

[1] Blackwood's Magazine, May 1886.

and it may perhaps be worth while to look at the 'Divina Commedia' from the standpoint of some of those who may come unaided to the attempt to understand the meaning—the simplest and most elementary meaning—of the world-famous work. The study of the great Italian, for some reason or other, frequently breeds a peculiar intellectual and spiritual exclusiveness. But this is no new feeling.

> "If Dante mourns, there wheresoe'er he be
> That such high fancies of a soul so proud
> Should be laid open to the vulgar crowd
> (As touching my discourse I'm told by thee),
> This were my grievous pain." [1]

So wrote Boccaccio to one who had censured his public exposition of Dante in 1373—fifty-two years after the great poet's death—and the year, too, of our own Chaucer's visit to Florence. But the genial story-teller need not have been afraid. No *great* poet's work really suffers from contact with the crowd. There will always be a large number of the uneducated ready to be touched by the best, however much they may miss the subtler delicacies of artistic work,—and it is impossible

[1] Dante and his Circle (D. G. Rossetti), p. 250.

for the most commonplace audience to harm a great writer; whilst, on the other hand, the greater the writer, the more certainty there is of his sowing seed of incalculable value in the minds of the most commonplace audience. In music, for example, it has often been observed that, in such assemblages as the People's Concerts, the greatest masters always make themselves felt, however much the general taste may have been debased by music-halls. It is said that in the art of acting, no player ever made a complete failure in the part of Hamlet, the play is so entrancing. In the sacred cabinet of the Sistine Madonna, the solemn awe is not confined to the cultured few. It is the possession and the privilege of the many. And is the same thing not true also of pure literature? The experiment will now, at any rate, be tried in rather a crucial case; for the 'Divine Comedy,' translated—and on the whole admirably well translated—by Longfellow, has been published in Professor Morley's 'Universal Library,' and can be bought for the modest sum of 10d.

It would be interesting (if it were possible) to know the numbers and the class of buyers of the book. There will undoubtedly be a number of artisans and mechanics among them. What will they think of it? It must be a considerable puzzle, viewed probably with mixed feelings. Professor Morley has given a succinct account of the poet and his writings in five pages of very small print, and then follows the introductory canto of the "Inferno" preluding the other 99 cantos—the mystic number of the great vision—without one single note or explanation of any kind whatever. It would probably have been quite impossible, as a question of expense, to have given the Italian text at the foot of the English version for the nominal price of a shilling; but will it not be necessary to publish another volume, in the original, if the book is to have a wide appreciation or success amongst the poorer of the English upper middle classes and the more advanced of the lower middle classes, for whom the series is mainly intended?

There is a good deal to be said in favour of the absence of notes. Adequate notes are necessarily so frequent, that the continuity of reading is too much interrupted for pleasure.

Very few of the buyers of such a book are likely to become Dante students, and whosoever listens with the right ear can enjoy the most exquisite bits of the poem without any explanation. But, apart from the original, the work cannot be fairly tasted in a translation. With an Italian grammar and dictionary, any intelligent person, fired with enthusiasm, can master the most beautiful passages in the original with the help of such a rendering as this of Longfellow's, and reading the poem in that way will be of the highest value. For when an Englishman with only a smattering of Italian asks himself why the reading of Dante gives him greater pleasure than almost anything known to him in his own language, one of the answers must be, that in the matter of *form* the great master writing 600 years ago has spoken the last word. But this pleasure can only be enjoyed (*savouré*, to use an expressive French word) by reading the very words that the poet himself has written. Lines so perfectly wrought as the story of Francesca da Rimini, the description of the voyage of Ulysses (which may be very profitably compared with Tennyson's transcript of it), the story of Ugolino, the meeting with Beatrice in purgatory, the picture of the bird waiting for the dawn, and the last canto of the "Paradiso," besides hundreds of other passages and single lines, "cannot be transmuted from their own speech to another without breaking all their sweetness and harmony."

There are single lines in Longfellow's translation which will appeal to every reader as admirably well given: for instance, Jason's desertion of Hypsipyle—

"Lasciolla quivi gravida e soletta;"—
"There did he leave her pregnant and forlorn;"[1]—

the line on Buonconte—

"Per una lagrimetta che 'l mi toglie;"—
"For one poor little tear that takes him from me"[2]—

or Virgil to Sordello—

"Non per far, ma per non fare ho perduto;"—
"I by not doing, not by doing lost," &c.[3]

In all of these the full flavour of the original is retained; and these are only a sample of many more of equal felicity. This little essay, however, is not meant for a criticism, but is

[1] Inf. xviii. 94.   [2] Purg. v. 107.   [3] Purg. vii. 25.

written on the assumption that the reader of the poem is trying to make what he can out of the one volume in his hands.

Probably few things in literature approach in exciting, breathless interest, the seven opening cantos of the "Inferno." They bear us so strongly along, that their effect is like the first sight of the ocean, of Niagara, or of the Alps,—amongst the three or four unforgettable impressions in life — amongst the three or four things much heard of which have not proved disappointments. If one had never known the name of Dante before reading them, one would still be enthralled, simply taking the words as they stand without any allegorical interpretation. The impressive opening—

"Nel mezzo del cammin di nostra vita
 Mi ritrovai per una selva oscura,
 Chè la diritta via era smarrita."

"Midway upon the journey of our life
 I found myself within a forest dark,
 For the straightforward pathway had been lost.'

The meeting with the shade of Virgil :—

"Or se' tu quel Virgilio, e quella fonte,
 Che spande di parlar sì largo fiume?"

The sense that such lines as the following have come echoing down to us through our own greatest poet in 'Hamlet':—

> "And as he is who unwills what he willed,
> And by new thoughts doth his intention change,
> So that from his design he quite withdraws;
> Such I became upon that dark hillside,
> Because in thinking I consumed the emprise
> Which was so very prompt in the beginning."

The appearance of Beatrice on the scene, and the exquisite passage where we are introduced by Lucia to the relation between her and Dante:—

> "Disse: Beatrice, loda di Dio vera,
> Chè non soccorri quei che t' amò tanto,
> Ch' uscìo per te della volgare schiera?"

> "'Beatrice,' said she, 'the true praise of God,
> Why succourest thou not him who loved thee so—
> For thee he issued from the vulgar herd?'"

The comparison of Dante's renovated courage to the flowerets:—

> "By nocturnal chill
> Bowed down and closed, when the sun whitens them
> Uplift themselves all open on their stems."

The descriptions of the starlings, of the cranes, and best of all, that of the doves:—

> "As turtle-doves called onward by desire,
>   With open and steady wings to the sweet nest
>   Fly through the air, by their volition borne."

The inscription on the Gate of Hell, "Lasciate ogni speranza, voi, ch' entrate," and the sadness of the blind life of those "who have foregone the good of intellect." The meeting with Homer and the Latin poets:—

> "Parlando cose che 'l tacere è bello."
> "Things saying 'tis becoming to keep silent."

And the picture of the great shades:—

> "People there were with solemn eyes and slow,
>   Of great authority in their countenance;
>   They spake but seldom, and with gentle voices.
>   . . . .
>   . . . . The mighty spirits
>   Whom to have seen I feel myself exalted."

Every word of canto v., with the story of Francesca da Rimini, especially that culminating line embodying the tragedy in half-a-dozen words:—

> "Quel giorno più non vi leggemmo avante."

The natural pitying feeling exhibited by Dante to Ciacco the glutton:—

> "Thy wretchedness
>   Weighs on me so, that it to weep invites me."

The great lines on Fortune :—

> "Now canst thou, son, behold the transient farce
>   Of goods that are committed unto Fortune
>   For which the human race each other buffet;
> For all the gold that is beneath the moon,
>   Or ever has been, of these weary souls
>   Could never make a single one repose."

And these on the sullen, which should be inscribed on all our hearts :—

> "Fitti nel limo dicon : Tristi fummo
>   Nell' aer dolce che da sol s' allegra,
>   Portando dentro accidioso fummo ;
> Or ci attristiam nella belletta negra."

> "Fixed in the mire they say we sullen were
>   In the sweet air which by the sun is gladdened,
>   Bearing within ourselves the sluggish reek ;
> *Now* we are sullen in this sable mire."

In truth, it may be said of these seven cantos as Alfieri said of the whole 'Comedy,' that one may begin by making extracts, but one ends by wishing to extract every word. The epithets are so original, " mute of all light," " where the sun is silent," the rain " eternal maledict and cold and heavy," " the air without a star," the " sound of hands," the " embrowned air," the " water sombre-hued." We have every finest quality of his style — the simplicity, the strength, the compression, the forthrightness, the tenderness; and we are altogether wrought up to the highest pitch of enthusiasm not only towards the poem, but towards the poet. No grating note has been sounded: so far the tone is sad, but it is solemn,—when it becomes passionate and personal, we feel inclined to echo Farinata's words—

"Come avesse lo Inferno in gran dispitto."

But the opening of the poem strikes exactly the right key. A deep awe has fallen upon us, and we are therefore in a state of mind to receive all the greater shock when we are suddenly brought face to face, in canto viii., with the brutality (there is no other word for it) of Dante's expressed delight in the torture of Philippo Argentí. We feel that we are in the hands of a different man from the author of the previous cantos, and we feel it with resentment—a resentment which we are intended to feel towards Argenti, but which we unfortunately do feel towards Dante for his want of self-control and want of dignity in the treatment of that "arrogant person," who, whatever he may have been in life, says here, appealingly, "Thou seest that I am one who weeps." A glory has passed away; and we can only account for the sudden change in the tone on the hypothesis that a considerable interval of time elapsed between the writing of the seventh and eighth cantos — a time during which the great tragedy in Dante's life occurred. From this point onward to the end of the "Inferno," the wrath is always gathering, — not only the righteous wrath against the worse forms of sin as the poet descends the circles of hell — where a good man might well say, "I do well to be angry" — but passionate personal attacks on wretched sinners, where the want of dignity in the narrator turns all our sympathies to the sinners; and perhaps, before going further, it will be well for a reader to familiarise himself with the history of the poet,—to try to find some of the reasons which prompted him to write as he has written.

There are authors so impersonal that we care not greatly to know them in their habits as they lived. Dante will be found to be, above all, personal. The little that is really known of him, from outside and contemporary sources, can be gathered up in very few words; but all his own writing is more or less autobiographical.

Of all poets that ever were born, he was perhaps the most favourably circumstanced in his birth and in his surroundings. Of good family, and with sufficient fortune, Durante Alighieri (as he was christened in 1265) received the usual education of a Florentine young man in his circumstances. There is absolutely no historical evidence to prove that he went to any of the universities to which his various biographers have consigned him; but we know from his own writing that he fell under the influence of Brunetto Latini, one of the most learned men of that time. Guido Cavalcanti, then the chief poet in Italy, was his elder by thirteen years, and the first among his friends. When, at the age of eighteen, the rising star writes his first sonnet, he sends it round to all the sonneteers of the day, and is at once received and welcomed as a poet among poets. There is no early struggle with self-education, with chill penury, or with an unsympathetic environment. From the age of nine he has made Beatrice Portinari his idol and his ideal, and has received that highest education which a pure young love can best give.

> "For indeed I know
> Of no more subtle master under heaven
> Than is a maiden passion for a maid."

She dies when he is twenty-five years old. He is disconsolate; takes his part in military service, and we have his own account of his sensations on two or three occasions,[1] when there were engagements of some importance. Afterwards he marries Madonna Gemma, of the family of the Donati, and five sons and one or two daughters are born to him. Having entered public life in those stormy times of feud and faction, he becomes one of the Priors or chief officers of the Republic; is sent many times on embassies by his Government (one of them giving occasion for the famous and very characteristic remark—" Se io vo, chi rimane? e se io rimango, chi va?"—" If I go, who is to remain; and if I remain, who is to go?"). From his last embassy to Pope Boniface VIII. he never returned to Florence, the party

[1] Inf. xxi. 94, xxii. 1-10; Purg. v. 93.

opposed to him having attained power, and in his absence decreed his banishment, with the unusually severe addition to the sentence that he should be burned alive if ever he returned to his native city. For the last nineteen years of his life he was a wanderer. In exile he died, even as in exile he had been conceived, for his father and mother were among the "fuorusciti" up to the time of his birth. Boccaccio describes him as of medium height, the face long, the nose aquiline, the jaw large, and the under lip protruding considerably over the upper, shoulders rather bent, eyes larger than ordinary, an olive complexion, hair and beard thick, crisp, and black; most temperate in eating and drinking, and most zealous in study or in any other pursuit, and he went along with the air of a melancholy man, and a dreamer. He had a lofty soul, and was excessively haughty.

Boccaccio's life of Dante has been too much decried. It is quite true that it is rhetorical, insufficient, often inaccurate as to dates, and generally very much below the level of its subject; but when the other biographers are consulted, almost all their salient points are referred back to Boccaccio. His description of Dante's first meeting with Beatrice, though taken from the 'Vita Nuova,' has a certain charm of its own in the Boccaccian style, which may be thus roughly transcribed:—

"It used to be the habit of the ladies and gentlemen of Florence, when the sweet springtime arrived, to give themselves up to social enjoyments, each in his own circle of society. Following this custom, a worthy citizen, Folco Portinari, had invited his neighbours to assemble at his house upon the first of May. Among the company was Alighieri, the father of Dante, who brought his boy, then scarcely nine years of age. And it happened that Bice, the daughter of Folco, was there too —a maiden not yet past her eighth year, graceful, charming, and attractive in her manners, of a beautiful countenance, and grave beyond her years. Her very delicate features were in admirable harmony, and over and above their beauty, revealed such candid charms, that by many she was said to be almost an angel. Dante's gaze was riveted on her with so great an affection, that, child though he was, he received her so deeply into his soul that no other after-pleasure ever effaced the lovely image. And this love not only persisted, but it increased to such a degree that Dante had no greater desire, and no greater consolation, than to see her who was its object. As he advanced in life, this passion very often occasioned him both sighs and tears, which are poured forth in his 'Vita Nuova.' It ought to be added that his love was a very pure love—which is rare in passions of this kind."

This, as we know, was the master—or the mistress—influence in Dante's life, and it is impossible to understand the 'Divina Commedia' without some theory regarding this relation to Beatrice. There can be no doubt of her existence in the flesh. There is no evidence that Dante ever wished to marry her. We know that she was married to Simone dei Bardi when our poet was twenty-two years old. But while she is a real woman, and we feel at times that it is a real passion, there is always a note of unreality in it. By the force of his imagination, and by his perfect art-workmanship, Dante has contrived to create and to sustain from the beginning to the end of his writing a relation so simple in appearance and so complex in fact, that it is always impossible to determine where the true Beatrice ends and the ideal begins. His passion (even in its least allegorical shape) is evidently not at any time a man's natural passion for the woman he is in love with. It is rather the intellectual and spiritual perception of what such a passion might be ideally. A flesh-and-blood woman — a child and then a woman—formed the basis of the sentiment, which could not have existed without that basis; but we continually feel that there is a good deal of reflex egoism about it. It could never have stood the strain of intimate acquaintance, — at close quarters it would have been shattered. A salutation in the street was sufficient to nourish it, and more might have proved dangerous. But over and above her influence as a woman, she represents in the 'Comedy,' allegorically, Heavenly Wisdom and Theology; and the suggestion may be hazarded that, between the real and the purely allegorical, Dante personifies his own better nature in Beatrice. She has become his outside conscience. Whenever he goes wrong in life, it is her whom he has offended. He can scarcely now be imagined apart from her. She reigns supreme as a vital part of himself, from the first word to the last. In words of the "Paradiso,"—

> "From the first day that I beheld her face
> In this life to the moment of this look,
> The sequence of my song has ne'er been severed." [1]

With this view of Beatrice—as representing Dante's own higher nature—it may be said that not even in Goethe himself was there greater warfare of two souls within one breast which could not be harmonised, — "the one which clung with indomitable energy to the earth and the things of earth, and the other which was ever struggling to rise beyond the confines of this world into the illimitable." Dante, in his dark strivings, is always conscious of the right way, and in the end his higher soul carries us with him on a magic cloak to the realms of Paradise. The interest of the drama, in the 'Comedy,' centres in the ascent of that soul of his. For the more we

---

[1] Par. xxx. 28.

read the poem, the more we feel that the most dominant note throughout is the author's personality; and one way of understanding its meaning is to conceive that the journey recorded in the vision is to be accounted for by Dante's own faithlessness, both in the flesh and in the spirit, to his ideal—to his own higher nature—to Beatrice. And if Dante was ever faithless to his ideal, how much more faithless are other mortals! This is one of the lessons we have to learn from the 'Comedy.' But it is all one long lesson—a long discipline. Keeping this in mind, let us now enter on the most difficult and the most delicate part of the subject.

Boccaccio was seven years old when Dante died. He was the intimate friend of Dante's nephew, and had therefore exceptional opportunities of knowing the truth. Moreover, he was the first person chosen to deliver public lectures on the 'Divina Commedia' in Florence, fifty years after Dante's death, so that it may be inferred that he was then considered thoroughly competent to deal with the subject; and this is what he writes in his 'Life,'—not lightly, or to round a period, but with a solemn appeal to Dante's shade:—

"Of a truth, I blush to cast any shadow on the bright reputation of so great a man; but as the order of my history began by setting forth his good qualities, the less that I try to conceal his frailties, the more will I be believed in what I have said in his praise. It is then to Dante himself that I address my excuses, if, perchance, from the heights of heaven, his scornful eye is looking at me now as I write. Along with all his strength of character and all his learning (and I have already shown how much of both he possessed), he was not free from the sway of the passions (*lussuria*)—nay, they had very great power over him, not only in his youth, but in his riper years; and such vice, however natural and common it may be, is certainly not to be commended. Nay, it is very difficult to plead a tolerable excuse for it."

Nor is this the only contemporary evidence. In a well-known sonnet, Guido Cavalcanti rebukes Dante for his way of life after the death of Beatrice.

"I come to thee by day-time constantly,
But in thy thoughts *too much of baseness find:*
Greatly it grieves me for thy gentle mind,

And for thy many virtues gone from thee.
It was thy wont to shun much company,
  Unto all sorry concourse ill inclined :
  And still thy speech of me heartfelt and kind,
Had made me treasure up thy poetry.
But now, I dare not, *for thine abject life,*
  Make manifest that I approve thy rhymes ;
    Now come I in such sort that thou mayst know,—
  Ah ! prithee read this sonnet many times.
So shall that evil one who bred this strife
  Be thrust from thy dishonoured soul and go." [1]

Dante himself, in speaking to Forese Donati, his brother-in-law, who was among the gluttons in the " Purgatorio," says :—

    " If thou bring back to mind
What thou with me hast been, and I with thee,
The present memory will be grievous still.
Out of that life he turned me back who goes
  In front of me—[Virgil].
    . . . .

His encouragements have led me up,
  Ascending and still circling round the mount
  That you doth straighten whom the world made crooked." [2]

We know that our poet himself had no tendency to the sin of gluttony. The passage must therefore refer to other lapses. It has

---

[1] Dante and his Circle (D. G. Rossetti, p. 161).
[2] Purg. xxiii. 115.

been attempted to explain all allusions of this sort by supposing them to be simply allegorical. Shakespeare has been treated in something of the same fashion. Is it not best, however, because truest, to acknowledge to ourselves that both of them were men with the strongest intellectual and spiritual natures, founded on strong animal natures (the conjunction is not unknown), with passions strong in proportion to their beings—passions that sometimes completely dominated them; that there were times in their lives when the unmanageable horse of the chariot plunged down and dragged the other after it? But their writings will not appeal the less to us on that account—nay, rather the more. One of our own great living poets has pointed out that one at any rate of the meanings of this mighty polysensuous work of Dante's is to show

"How men may rise on stepping-stones
Of their dead selves to higher things."

Among mortals, it is not the faultless beings but the faulty, who have conquered and triumphed over their faults, that have left the greatest heritage of good to mankind. For their lesson is, that no sinner who has the root of goodness and of nobleness and of purity in his heart, need ever despair while life lasts of coming "quando che sia alle beate genti"—may always hope that for him, too, there is the water of Lethe from which he may emerge after he has paid the penalty of his faults with tears,

"Pure and disposed to mount unto the stars."

Before proceeding with the "Inferno," let us read carefully cantos xxx. and xxxi. of the "Purgatorio," and perhaps we may then feel that we hold in our hands one of the keys to "the straight way which was lost." It is the great scene of Dante's first meeting with Beatrice—one of the very grandest passages in the whole comedy—and of course it ought to be read in its entirety. Unfortunately space forbids anything but an extract here. She speaks—

"But still that thou mayst feel a greater shame
For thy transgression, and another time
Hearing the Sirens thou mayst be more strong,"[1]

---

[1] Cf. Purg. xix. 7-32 and 58-60; also Purg. xxxi. 80-90. See, too, Inf. xviii. 127-137, and Letter to Moruello Malaspina, dated, Witte thinks, in 1310, in which Dante writes how "Love terrible and imperious" has him in its power and reigns over him, and that his principles are of no avail against it.

"Cast down the seed of weeping and attend;
    So shalt thou hear how in an opposite way
    My buried flesh should have directed thee.
Never to thee presented art or nature
    Pleasure so great as the fair limbs wherein
    I was enclosed, which scattered are in earth.
And if the highest pleasure then did fail thee
    By reason of my death, what *mortal* thing
    Should then have drawn thee into its desire?
    . . . .
Thou oughtest not to have stooped thy pinion downward
    To wait for further blows, or little girl,
    Or other vanity of such brief use.
    . . . .
    . . . . . If thou
In hearing sufferest pain, lift up thy beard,
And thou shalt feel a greater pain in seeing.
    . . . .
Then I upraised at her command my chin,
    And when she by the beard the face demanded,
    Well I perceived the venom of her meaning."[1]

The allusion to the beard is a characteristically feminine way of making his peccadilloes unpleasant to the mature offender. Dante was forty-five years old in 1310. One hears the very voice of a real woman in the words, charged with jealousy and hurt feeling. They are spoken in a tone that we can scarcely

[1] Purg. xxxi. 43-75.

conceive the most highly imaginative poet putting in the mouth of an abstraction (call it Heavenly Wisdom, Theology, or what we will), who is supposed to address a disciple merely gone astray in philosophy, religion, or politics. The allusion to her own fair limbs, and to the *mortal* thing which had drawn Dante into its desire—not to mention the use of the word "pargoletta"—seems to be conclusive.

And Beatrice shows us the pity of it—

"By the largess of celestial graces
. . . .
Such had this man become in his new life,
Potentially, that every righteous habit
Would have made admirable proof in him;
But so much more malignant and more savage
Becomes the land untilled and with bad seed
The more good earthly vigour it possesses.
. . . .
So low he fell that all appliances
For his salvation were already short,
Save showing him the people of perdition."

Let us now try to familiarise ourselves with the atmosphere in which the young poet, blessed by the "largess of celestial graces," and so full of gentleness, apparently, in his spring-time, sang his quaint mystic ballad of the New or the Early Life. In reading it, we can only think, in his own words, of the olden times—

"The dames and cavaliers, the toils and ease
That filled our souls with love and courtesy."[1]

But this was far indeed from the actual condition of Florence in the years which followed—1287-1300. The little city could put 30,000 men under arms within its walls; and we read of constant unintermitting feuds between family and family, between house and house—a close-packed fighting neighbourhood, that must have been a very lively sample of the Inferno. Taking Dante's own house in the Via San Martino as a centre, we are amazed to see what a tiny circle includes the ancient city with "il mio bel San Giovanni" (the Baptistery); the Badia, whence the bell tolled the *terza e nona*; Santa Maria Novella, where Cimabue's great picture of the Virgin was carried in triumph; Or San Michele; the yet unfinished Duomo and Giotto's rising campanile; the Palazzo Vecchio and Santa Croce

[1] Purg. xiv. 109-111.

still a-building. The blue sky, the bright sun, the peculiarly clear and thrilling air, the opalescent light which makes every building a poem in Florence, are all the same to-day as they were 600 years ago—made to fashion a poet. The lot of the masses, chattering and chaffering in the market-place, or thronging the noisy Calimara, is probably not very different now. The poor have become not much less poor, but the rich have perhaps become relatively less rich—for the City of Flowers was then the chief banking centre of Europe, and her palaces remain the monuments of the capitalists—mostly extinct volcanoes now, as are her famous citizens.

As we look down from the heights of San Miniato or Bellosguardo, the wonder grows how one such very little spot on the earth's surface could have produced in three short centuries (thirteenth to sixteenth) so many names eminent in history, and that within its walls it could have held at one and the same time (while Roger Bacon was finishing his work in England and Sir William Wallace was the glory of Scotland) men of such mark as Cimabue, Brunetto Latini, Guido Cavalcanti, Casella, Arnolfo, Dante, Giotto, Dino Frescobaldi, R. Malaspina, Dino Compagni, and Giovanni Villani—all in the full vigour of their manhood and of their work. Every stone speaks to us of the great dead; and if the men were worthy of the city, the city in its beauty was becoming worthy of the men. For surely it is, as old Boccaccio has somewhere described it, " Di ogni città d'Italia bellissima." Here it was with Fiesole above him, the purple hills beyond, Monte Morello near, and Falterona in the distance, with "il bel fiume d'Arno" flowing through the vale, that this young eagle of song mewed his mighty youth. This was the stage on which he played his part—an active part—from his 25th to his 36th year—up to " the middle of the way of life,"—battling in the midst of the seething politics of the city for the four last years of that period. Without this experience of the active life, the 'Divina Commedia' could never have been written; but if the poet had remained a politician, " the straight way" would indeed have been lost, and the great vision would have been lost too. Dante's banishment, which to himself and to his friends no doubt at the time seemed to be the extinguishing of his career — his failure as a public man, as a politician — was really, as we see it now, the necessary condition for his arriving at that perpetuation of his fame the desire for which no doubt was innate, but which, he himself tells us, had first been taught to him by Brunetto Latini—*come uom' s'eterna*. It was not only that he widened the horizon of his view of life in his travels, but that he was able more or less to liberate his soul from personal participation in all the miserable petty jealousies of the time; for no party politician, however great by nature, can ever be at his best. Dante's contributions to politics are the great thoughts of an ideal, not of a practical, politician—pregnant ideas of a universal spiritual and a universal political direction. The Pope is his "sun" and the Emperor his "moon," both divinely ordained.

Such a work as the 'Divina Commedia,' with a scope so vast and a treatment so elaborate, demanded the sacrifice of a life. The extraordinary compression of the thought, the variety and the intensity of the imagery, the mass of historical and mythical allusions and their exactitude, required a mind wholly disengaged from the ordinary business of the world; and it ought to be recognised that his exile, although the bitterest trial in his earthly life, has been the means of securing his true immortality as nothing else could have done. The 'Divina Commedia' alone has made him eternal. All his other writings together might have secured him a place in the first class among the great, but far, indeed, from the place he holds as one of the universally acknowledged triumvirate of the world's literature.

Contemporaries can never realise the relative importance of the personages as they play their parts on the stage: the politicians and the soldiers always stand out in grotesque relief. To the Florentines of 1300 (even to such a man as Giovanni Villani), the Uberti, the Donati, the Cerchi, and the rest of the powerful local families, were the only actors worth talking about: whereas to the mass of the men of our time, Dante the great poet, and Giotto the great painter, are the real "people of importance." Where are they all now who were contemporaries with Dante in his political career? To the million readers of to-day no vestige of them remains, except such immortality as he has given them in his rhyme. To remain a politician was to kill a poet: and we must remember that Dante was not only a great poet, but he was also a great philosopher, a great theologian. In the "Paradise" we read how, as his higher nature emerges, he becomes conscious of the degrading influences of the political life from which he had escaped:—

"O thou insensate care of mortal men,
   How inconclusive are the syllogisms
   That make thee beat thy wings in downward flight!
One after laws and one to aphorisms
   Was going, and one following the priesthood,
   And one to reign by force or sophistry,
And one in theft and one in state affairs,
   One in the pleasures of the flesh involved,
   Wearied himself, one gave himself to ease;
When I from all these things emancipate
   With Beatrice above there in the heavens,
   With such exceeding glory was received!" [1]

And here we have another key to the "straight way which was lost."

But this sense of emancipation only came

---

[1] Par. xi. 1-12.

later, with the years that bring the philosophic mind. In his first hot rage at the peculiar severity of his sentence of banishment, we become aware of the savage unforgiving side of the poet's nature. There probably was always a good deal of truth in Cecco Angioleri's line—

"Sugar he seems, but salt's in all his ways."

From the 8th canto onwards in the "Inferno," we seem to see him ever in imagination sweeping, in his stately eagle flight, over Florence, poising on slow broad wings, with eyes so keen that nothing escaped them—with beak and talons always ready to pounce on any miscreant on earth—eager to rend and pick him to pieces (with a certain bird of prey delight); yet still, when the higher spirit willed, always able to fly up again into the very fountain of light. With a character that, alas! often repels, and an intellect that always fascinates us, he stands out in the twenty-five last cantos of the "Inferno" as the cruellest of poets in his judgments and in his treatment of men; and yet often, in the same canto, the tenderest in his interpretations of nature.

There is a certain pathos in Boccaccio's somewhat imaginative account of the circumstances which divided the seven opening cantos from the remainder of the poem :—

"At the very time when Dante was most busily engaged on this glorious labour (after he had composed seven out of the hundred cantos which he had determined on), came the grave incident of his expulsion or flight, which led him to abandon all his projects. He was adrift, and obliged to wander during many years. But the accomplishment of the will of God cannot be counteracted by a stroke of bad fortune. So that it happened that some of his family, looking by chance for some papers in his strong-boxes, found a little copy-book in which the seven cantos were written. It had been put there in a place of safety at the time when the ungrateful populace had risen against our poet, and, more intent on plunder than on just vengeance, had made a raid on his house. The cantos were read with admiration, and the finders, not knowing what they had got hold of, carried the book to one of our fellow-citizens, Dino di Messer Lambertuccio Frescobaldi, who was famous at that time for his recitation of poems.

The moment Dino cast his eyes over the little book, he was so much struck with the beauty of the style, as well as with the depth of thought which seemed to him to lie hidden under the beautiful crust of words, that he came to the conclusion at once that it was Dante's work. Distressed to see the poem unfinished, and finding that Dante was staying at the time with the Marquis Moruello Malaspina, he communicated to the Marquis the circumstances of the discovery, and his desire to see the work continued.

"The Marquis was a man of high culture, and when he had read the cantos with great admiration he showed them to Dante, asking him if he knew who the author might be. Dante recognised them, and replied at once that they were his. Then the Marquis begged him not to leave unfinished a work so well begun. 'Of a truth,' said Dante, 'I had thought that these verses had been lost in my ruin with the rest of my books; and partly from this belief, and partly from the constant fatigues which I have undergone in exile, I had entirely abandoned the idea of finishing the lost work. But as these cantos have been recovered so unexpectedly, and as you seem to wish it, I will try to remember my original plan, and if I succeed I will continue the work.'

"We can readily imagine," continues Boccaccio, "that he had no great difficulty in recovering the thread of his original idea; and it is in taking up this thread again that he opens the 8th canto with the words: ' Io dico seguitando che assai prima,' &c. ('I say, continuing,' &c.), from which, when we have the clue, it is evident that this is the resumption of the interrupted work."

Assuming that there is a little basis of fact in this account, it furnishes us with an hypothesis which enables us to understand better how the bitterness of unmerited misfortune was working a change in Dante's nature—or rather, was temporarily operating to bring out the worse side of it. For the more we try to figure to ourselves and to grasp his real character, the more we realise the anguish that his proud disdainful spirit must have been constantly undergoing in a dependent position. We feel how the iron entered into his soul. It must have been a veritable crucifixion for him—

> "And that which most shall weigh upon thy shoulders
> Will be the bad and foolish company
> With which into this valley thou shalt fall." [1]

The patronage of Can Grande must have become insufferable. Grand seigneur and fine fellow when he had everything his own way, there was also a good deal of the spoilt child of fortune in him. The world's admiration for the splendid courage with which Dante finished his work, bowed down under the weight of such a load, has contributed to his undying renown. No doubt he had himself in mind when he wrote of the pilgrim Romeo—

> "E se il mondo sapesse il cuor ch' egli ebbe,
> Mendicando sua vita a frusto a frusto,
> Assai lo loda, e più lo loderebbe."

> "And if the world could know the heart he had
> In begging, bit by bit, his livelihood,
> Though much it laud him it would laud him more." [2]

The allusions to his exile are constant in his writings, and very touching: "I have compassion for all unhappy people, but my greatest compassion is reserved for those who, eating out their hearts in exile, see their native land only in their dreams."

[1] Par. xvii. 61.   [2] Par. vi. 140.

But it is only in the most rarely tempered natures that the uses of adversity sweeten the disposition. They turn the unforgiving to gall. Dante's was never the spirit to forgive or to forget. Whilst it may be admitted that no one has ever clutched more firmly in an iron grasp the letter of the Christian religion, — its doctrines — its evidences (as understood in the fourteenth century),—it may, perhaps, without presumption, be permitted us to doubt whether in his writings he exhibits an equally true appreciation of the real nature — of the true essence — of Christ's gospel. He is constantly referred to as the pre-eminently Christian poet; but does he not really belong to the Hebrew type —the type of David, Isaiah, Jeremiah? An eye for an eye, and a tooth for a tooth, is his avowed doctrine. He is above all things a Roman—a Churchman of the true Church —with a leaning to St Dominic, of whom he says—

"Therein was born the amorous paramour
  Of Christian faith, the athlete consecrate,
    Kind to his own, and cruel to his foes."[1]

---

[1] Par. xii. 55.

He places the Inquisitor in heaven, and would have placed John Wesley in a very low circle of hell. He is an aristocrat in feeling—exclusive in all his tendencies. We can see very few rays of Christ's spirit, and can catch very little echo of His voice in Dante's judgments of sin, or in his general attitude towards life. There is no exaltation of the humble and meek, but, on the contrary, something very like intellectual arrogance. In the "Paradise" he takes cognisance of—

> "Only the souls that unto fame are known,
> Because the spirit of the hearer rests not,
>   Nor doth confirm its faith by an example,
>   Which has the root of it unknown and hidden,
> Or other reason which is not apparent." [1]

This is not the spirit of the friend of publicans and sinners. Dante's is not a gospel for little children : as Villani says of him, "On account of his learning, he was a little haughty and shy and disdainful, and, like a philosopher almost ungracious, knew not well how to deal with unlettered folk." Those who are in the "piccioletta barca" are warned off in the second canto of the "Paradise"

[1] Par. xvii. 138.

from attempting to follow "behind my ship that singing sails along." It would be difficult to imagine Dante saying to a woman taken in adultery, "Go and sin no more;" or to her accusers, "Let him that is without sin cast the first stone at her." He does not act on the injunction, "Judge not, that ye be not judged." He never has a doubt about his own competence to sit in judgment on the whole human race — past, present, and future — and not only on the race, but on named individuals, which is a much more dangerous pretension. His precepts are better than his practice—

"And you, O mortals, hold yourselves restrained in judging."[1]

To us general readers, 600 years after the event, the names of Brunetto Latini and of Guido Guinicelli, "the father of me and of my betters," have become mere types,—any other names would be equally effective to point a moral or adorn a tale; but when we consider that these men were quite recently dead, and that their relatives and friends

[1] Par. xx. 133.

were still alive when the 'Divina Commedia' was published — that they were both men to whom Dante acknowledged that he was immensely indebted intellectually and spiritually—the gibbeting of the one in the "Inferno" and the other in the "Purgatorio" for very heinous sins makes us stand aghast. It is not a sufficient explanation that it was 600 years ago — other times other manners. A natural and proper reverence for Dante as one of the greatest moralising and spiritualising influences in the world leads us at first naturally, though perhaps unreasonably, to expect that under all circumstances and at all times he will himself, in his own conduct, prove true to the fundamental principles of all morality — a sense of justice and of charity as well as of severity. Some one has described the virtuous man to be one who has always a severe standard for his own conduct, and the most lenient that the circumstances will admit for his neighbour's —"using his imagination in the service of charity." It may be said, "Judex damnatur cum nocens absolvitur." Be it. But then the guilt must always be publicly proved.

It must not rest on the mere *ipse dixit* even of a poet, however eminent; otherwise all our sympathies go out to the "cara buona imagine paterna," and to "il padre mio e degli altri miei miglior," and no good is done to us by their example; but we can fancy the evil done in Florence, at the time, by this outrage on the memory of the accused, who were no longer there to answer for themselves,—by the cruel pain inflicted on their friends. In the case of these two famous writers and of the two citizens "who were so worthy"—Tegghiaio Aldobrandi and Jacopo Rusticucci—one of two things. Either their offences had been proved and were matter of common knowledge, or they were not. If they *were*, there would have been some justification for selecting their names, as the accused must have had an opportunity of clearing their characters, if that were possible, during their lifetime. But if their offences were *not* definitely, absolutely, publicly proved beyond possibility of doubt, it would be very difficult to make out a case to justify the mention of their names. There is unfortunately no want of *types*. It does not seem as if Dante himself could have had proofs of their guilt, because in a previous circle he asks Ciacco where these very men were "who on good deeds set their thoughts"—

"Say where they are, and cause that I may know them;
    For great desire constraineth me to learn,
    If heaven doth sweeten them or hell envenom."[1]

And when he does come upon them, his relation of the scene is very curious. After poor Rusticucci has complained, "My savage wife more than aught else doth harm me," Dante continues—

"Could I have been protected from the fire,
    Below I should have thrown myself among them,
    And think the Teacher would have suffered it.
But as I should have burned and baked myself,
    My terror overmastered my goodwill,
    Which made me greedy of embracing them," &c.[2]

. . . .

"I of your city am; and evermore
    *Your labours and your honourable names
    I with affection have retraced and heard.*"[3]

Then he breaks out into one of his tirades against Florence: the shades pay him a pretty compliment—"looked at each other as one looks at truth"—and he leaves them.

[1] Inf. vi. 82.   [2] Inf. xvi. 46.   [3] Inf. xvi. 58.

Even his most fanatical devotees draw the line at Dante's treatment of Guido of Montefeltro, who, after being honourably mentioned in the 'Convito' as "this most noble Latin," is ignominiously consigned to the eighth circle of hell for giving most dastardly advice to Boniface VIII. It is believed that there is absolutely no historical evidence to confirm the acusation. Muratori suggests that political motives probably furnish the key. The imputation of motives is justified by these unsustained accusations. Dante's prophetic soul, perhaps, had in view a Muratori (but did not quite see the look he would give) in the lines—

"Ah me! how very cautious men should be
With those who not alone behold the act,
But with their wisdom look into the thoughts!"[1]

If anything were wanted to prove the demoralising effect on any human being of setting himself up in the position of the Almighty as the eternal judge of other individual and contemporary men's sins, it would be found in the crescendo movement in Dante's personal cruelty in the descriptions of the

[1] Inf. xvi. 118.

"Inferno"—from the most ignoble and ghastly gambols in the "new sport" with the Malebranche, the episode of Vanni Fucci and the serpents,—"From that time forth the serpents were my friends,"—the cowardly attack on Bocca degli Abati—pulling shocks of his hair out — to the culminating point where our Christian poet shows himself at once cruel and a traitor in his treatment of the shade of Friar Alberigo, who says in his frozen helplessness—

> "But hitherward stretch out thy hand forthwith,
> Open mine eyes; and open them I did not,
> And to be rude to him was courtesy."[1]

And this after having made a solemn compact with the shade—

> "If thou wouldst have me help thee,
> Say who thou wast; and if I free thee not,
> May I go to the bottom of the ice."[2]

There can be no comment on this passage—except, perhaps, to admit that with a widening psychology we are forced to the conclusion that the greatest minds, the most noble spirits, often carry within themselves volcanic intensity of passion for evil as well as for good.

[1] Inf. xxxiii. 148.   [2] Inf. xxxiii. 116.

It may be supposed that on re-reading these lines, and leaving them to stand for all time, Dante had the same feeling towards them that he must have had to the passionate passage in the 'Convito,' where he says that to arguments against the immortality of the soul, "one would wish to reply not with words, but with a knife." This, though intense, is not really so malignant, because the eyes of the contemporary, who did not take precisely Dante's view of the most knotty of all problems, not being frozen, he might have had the chance of defending himself. These expressions must of course be taken figuratively. No actual bloodshed or broken bones were to be apprehended! But this intense way of arguing is open to objections. Seriously, these personal attacks, even on the most flagrant, the most contemptible, and the most hateful of sinners (who, be it remembered, are already undergoing eternal torments of unutterable anguish), must be acknowledged as below the dignity of a great poem and a great poet. Our first feeling is to draw a veil over all these ungoverned outbursts; but the after and perhaps more reasonable feeling is the wish to know the man Dante as he was, with all his faults. He is great enough to carry them. His very faults are part—perhaps an inseparable part—of that intensity of nature which is the secret of his power; but do not let us be misled into making virtues of his vices because he is Dante.

And it does not meet the case to say that because "these things are an allegory," or because Friar Alberigo was really still alive in the body, and it was only his soul that was already in hell, therefore Dante's behaviour on such occasions gives us no opportunity of judging his own nature. The essential quality of all allegory—and particularly of the allegory in the 'Divina Commedia'—is that it produces on us the most complete impression of reality. This is the very reason of its being, and the source of all its power. It is like reading a record of facts. Whoever undertakes to exhibit that most complex abstraction, a sinful human soul, in the concrete image of a body in torment, will necessarily be judged more or less by the way in which he deals with that image. Dante's treatment is constantly remorseless and vindictive. His worshippers resent this view, and will see no spot upon their sun. There seems to be a peculiar difficulty in writing on the subject with moderation, but there surely must be some mean between the flippant falsities of Voltaire that "Dante's reputation will go on increasing because scarcely anybody reads him," and the tone of the prostrate ones who are not content that the world should see anything less in their idol than "the pure severity of perfect light." These two points of view represent the misers and the prodigal in praise. "Perché tieni? e perché burli?" Does not the truth lie between them? and was not our poet really a man of supremest faculty, with one side of his nature noble, tender, godlike—the other side passionate, vindictive, demonic? He himself gives us one of the best clues to his own character in the lines—

"I who by nature am
Exceeding mutable in every guise."[1]

He was not one man, but half-a-dozen men rolled into one. But whether we regard him as one man or as six, we never get rid of his

[1] Par. v. 98.

unconscious and unconscionable egoism. Not only in the 'Divina Commedia,' but from the first word of the 'Vita Nuova' to the last word of the Sonnet addressed to Giovanni Quirino, Dante can never be said, in his verses, to get outside of his own personality. Every one has noticed his want of humour, but no one (so far as we know) has attributed it to this cause. Inordinate egoism and humour are mutually exclusive. In the 'Comedy' there is one faint gleam in the meeting with Statius in purgatory, which is charmingly described:—

> "These words towards me made Virgilius turn
>   With looks that in their silence said, 'Be silent!'
>   But yet the power that wills cannot do all things;
> For tears and laughter are such pursuivants
>   Unto the passion from which each springs forth,
>   In the most truthful least the will they follow.
> I only smiled as one who gives the wink;
>   Whereat the shade was silent, and it gazed
>   Into mine eyes, where most expression dwells;
> And, 'As thou well mayst consummate a labour
>   So great,' it said, 'why did thy face just now
>   Display to me the lightning of a smile?'
> Now am I caught on this side and on that;
>   One keeps me silent, one to speak conjures me,
>   Wherefore I sigh, and I am understood.
> 'Speak,' said my Master, 'and be not afraid

Of speaking, but speak out, and say to him
What he demands with such solicitude.'
Whence I: 'Thou peradventure marvellest,
O antique spirit, at the smile I gave;
But I will have more wonder seize upon thee.
This one, who guides on high these eyes of mine,
Is that Virgilius from whom thou didst learn
To sing aloud of men and of the gods.
If other cause thou to my smile imputedst,
Abandon it as false, and trust it was
Those words which thou hast spoken concerning him.'
Already he was stooping to embrace
My Teacher's feet; but he said to him: 'Brother,
Do not; for shade thou art, and shade beholdest.'
And he uprising: 'Now canst thou the sum
Of love which warms me to thee comprehend,
When this our vanity I disremember,
Treating a shadow as substantial thing.'"[1]

But the other instances of humour that have been laboriously culled are either very far-fetched or very grim. Wherever he goes, through hell, purgatory, or paradise, he is generally himself the gracious and benignant creature that the spirits dwelling in those parts are chiefly concerned about. They prophesy his future, and there is no want of self-appreciation in the terms of the prophecies. As Giuliani has said, Dante is the "protagonist" of his own comedy. In the 'Vita

[1] Purg. xxi. 103 *et seq.*

Nuova,' when Beatrice dies our poet quotes
Jeremiah: "How doth the city sit solitary,
that was full of people! How is she become a
widow, she that was great among the nations!"
And the attitude of his mind towards the pil-
grims is thoroughly characteristic. Here there
is real humour in the want of humour. We
never have a word about the glories of his
native city—of that Florence where Giotto
and Arnolfo were all the time busily at work
leaving behind them those art-treasures which
make the latter part of the thirteenth and the
earlier part of the fourteenth centuries so
unspeakably precious. We should never be
able to guess from Dante's verses that buildings were rising during his lifetime as im-
perishable as his own poems, and the spirit of
the citizens must have been far indeed from
wholly bad that has left behind such a record
in stone and in marble. The city having be-
haved unjustly and cruelly to its greatest man,
its greatest man cannot forgive the wrong;
nor can he get outside of himself sufficiently
to see that there were redeeming qualities in
the citizens. He turns off Cimabue and Giotto
in one triplet, and in the next triplet lets the

two Guidos know their place. He can find no one good enough to associate with in political life, and must make "a party by himself." No mention is anywhere made of wife or child in the 'Comedy'; and it may be noted that in all the references to children, it is the child's love for the mother, or the mother's love for the child, that is dwelt upon—showing the keen observation of the intellect, but not the instinct of the heart. It may be doubted, with all Dante's powers, whether he could have written the line—

"With light upon him from his Father's eyes."

Even in the Ugolino story, it is the children's feeling for their father more than the father's for the children that is prominent. Very noteworthy, too, is the difference in the treatment by Dante of his own offences compared with the offences of his fellow-mortals. His own passage through the fire is exceedingly short, but the unpleasantness of it is characteristically described:—

"When I was in it, into molten glass
   I could have cast me to refresh myself,
   So without measure was the burning there."[1]

---

[1] Purg. xxvii. 49.

He has Virgil in front and Statius behind to keep him company and to sustain his spirits. For himself, he feels that this penalty of a few minutes is adequate; but for the rest of the sinners,—for Homer, Virgil, and the other Latin poets,—he is content that for eternity they should linger—

"Where without hope they live on in desire;"

and for Brunetto Latini and the rest, eternal fire.

Almost every mention of Florence — and indeed of Italy — throughout the poem, is couched in the bitterest terms. Nine years after he had been exiled, he writes a letter to the Emperor Henry VII., which ought to be read by all who wish to know the full orb of Dante's character—the shadow as well as the light. Henry VII. really did a great deal more harm than good to Italy. He was a man of no practical capacity. He substituted for the respected Podestàs petty tyrants more or less hated, to whom he sold, at the highest price, the title of his vicars. He extorted money from the hostile towns, and begged it from the friendly towns. The

Marquis of Monferrat bought from him the privilege of coining debased money. Yet no terms of adulation are too strong for Dante in addressing him. He speaks of Florence as the viper that rushes at the bosom of her mother; the diseased sheep that contaminates by its touch the herd of the Lord; the wicked and impious Myrrha, whom he urges Henry to crush. All his letters at this time "To the Princes and People of Italy," and "To the most wicked Florentines in the City," are surcharged with bitterness, — "O most arrogant among the Tuscan peoples,—insensate both by natural and by acquired vices," &c., &c. To avenge himself and reinstate himself in power, it is difficult to say where he would have stopped short. He is sometimes cited as the Bard who saw in prophetic vision United Italy as we see it to-day. But King Humbert's position is scarcely that of the German Albert whom Dante demanded. He may bestride the saddle-bow, but he cannot use the spurs. A monarch who is a mere figurehead, registering the decrees of a legislature elected by universal suffrage, is about as far removed from Dante's ideal as light from darkness. The advocate of Cæsarism would scarcely wish to be credited with any share in the Garibaldian birth, which is in fact one of the legitimate offspring of the new democracy with which our age has been in travail since the French Revolution, whether for good or for ill.

Comparisons between one great poet and another are always futile; but to many Englishmen, who are not absolute devotees, but who yet feel the tremendous pressure of Dante's power, there must be a certain sense of relief in passing from the study of his work (particularly the latter part of the "Inferno") to that of Shakespeare for example. It is like passing from a cell where, amidst the fumes of incense, a great soul is communing with himself on all the irredeemable faults and follies of his fellow-creatures and on his own manifold virtues, to the bright bracing fresh air of the mountains, in the companionship of a healthy, human, natural, broadly-humorous man, delighting in his kind, and in full sympathy with all the various aspects of humanity—its comedy as well as its tragedy—and above all with its natural as well as its supernatural relations. But although the average man will generally feel that the concentrated essence of Dante's food is too strong for him, he will never, having once tasted it, cease to return again and again to that rich banquet. It is partly the poet's very egoism which causes his writing to come down to us after six centuries as if it had been written yesterday. He will always remain modern, for he has written all from himself. We constantly feel how much he is taking out of himself. We bend with him under the weight on his shoulders, acknowledging that he is not a pilot, "Ch'a sè medesmo parca." And we scarcely require to be told that for years the sacred poem made him lean. It almost makes us lean merely to contemplate it. Side by side with much that is repulsive in the latter part of the "Inferno," there are in almost every canto those wonderful descriptions of natural phenomena, those subtle observations of the habits of men and of their countenances, those dramatic incidents (in which our poet is always one of the chief actors), those allusions to his travels, those masterly "applications of ideas to life." Gozzi has somewhere said that "Danteide" would be the best title for the poem.

It is as true to-day as in 1300 that

"Avarice afflicts the world,
Trampling the good and lifting the depraved." [1]

And that—

"'Now it behoves thee thus to put off sloth,'
My Master said; 'for sitting upon down
Or under quilt, one cometh not to fame,
Withouten which whoso his life consumes
Such vestige leaveth of himself on earth,
As smoke in air, or in the water foam.'" [2]

Or—

"When now unto that portion of mine age
I saw myself arrived, when each one ought
To lower the sails, and coil away the ropes." [3]

How sad that this sound advice should be forgotten by so many of our day!

And to our generation of scandalmongers, how dignified and excellent is this reproof:—

"In listening to them was I wholly fixed,
When said the Master to me: 'Now just look,
For little wants it that I quarrel with thee.'
When him I heard in anger speak to me,
I turned me round towards him with such shame
That still it eddies through my memory.

---

[1] Inf. xix. 104. [2] Inf. xxiv. 46. [3] Inf. xxvii. 79.

And as he is who dreams of his own harm,
  Who dreaming, wishes it may be a dream,
  So that he craves what is, as if it were not;
Such I became, not having power to speak
  For to excuse myself I wished, and still
  Excused myself, and did not think I did it.
' Less shame doth wash away a greater fault,'
  The Master said, ' than this of thine has been;
  Therefore thyself disburden of all sadness,
And make account that I am aye beside thee,
  If e'er it come to pass that fortune bring thee
  Where there are people in a like dispute;
For a base wish it is to wish to hear it.'"

" Chè voler ciò udire è bassa voglia." [1]

Amidst all the gruesomeness and the horrors of the passage through hell, the relation to Virgil is always a delightfully refreshing human element in the journey. We have already alluded to the description of the first meeting, and there is a pretty acknowledgment later on by the Latin poet of his disciple's intimate acquaintance with all his work:—

" Ben lo sai tu, che la sai tutta quanta." [2]

And the parting in the " Purgatorio " is very simple and very touching.[3] On Dante's side

[1] Inf. xxx. 130-148. [2] Inf. xx. 114.
[3] Purg. xxx. 49-51.

there is always present the love of the Son for the Father, of the pupil for the master, of the inferior for the superior—the last a relation which the judgment of the world has somewhat changed. The "Inferno" closes with the appropriately lurid light of the Ugolino story—the most powerful and the most horrible in all poetry — and the description of Dis, where Dante in one of his marvellously descriptive lines says—

"Io non morii, e non rimasi vivo."
"I did not die, and I alive remained not."[1]

It may perhaps be said that by us—"the general"—the "Purgatorio" is always likely to be the best loved of the three canticles. To appreciate *all* of the "Paradiso," there must be a certain mystical tendency in us. To the majority of minds, it is the positive side of Dante's poetry that will be the most attractive — the scientific observation of man and nature more than the purely mystical imagination. In the "Purgatorio" we come back to the Dante of the seven opening cantos of the "Inferno"—full of sweetness and light,

[1] Inf. xxxiv. 25.

of dignity and solemnity. We are conscious of the old delight—

"D' antico amor senti' la gran potenza"—

in pressing on to each new beauty.

"He seeketh liberty, which is so dear."

We can only run over a few of the most famous passages. The meeting with "my own Casella," who has the good taste to sing one of Dante's own songs without so much as asking "What shall it be?" (a foolish query which some readers aloud have asked a more modern bard, and always get the natural answer, "Oh, I don't mind, as long as it's something of my own")—the second description of the doves collecting grain or tares, and of the sheep coming out from the fold—

"Timidly, holding down their eyes and nostrils,
And what the foremost does the others do,
Huddling themselves against her, if she stop
Simple and quiet, and the wherefore know not."[1]

The glorious lines put in the mouth of Manfred—

"But infinite Goodness hath such ample arms,
That it receives whatever turns to it."[2]

---

[1] Purg. iii. 79.   [2] Purg. iii. 122.

The description of the ascending soul—
> "Questa montagna è tale,
> Che sempre al cominciar di sotto è grave,
> E quanto uom più va sù, e men fa male."
>
> "This mount is such, that ever
> At the beginning down below 'tis tiresome,
> And aye the more one climbs the less it hurts."[1]

The flood of light we have here on Dante's character—
> "Mine eyes I turned at utterance of these words,
> And saw them watching with astonishment,
> But me, but me, and the light which was broken!
> 'Why doth thy mind so occupy itself,'
> The Master said, 'that thou thy pace doth slacken?
> What matters it to thee what here is whispered?
> Come after me, and let the people talk;
> Stand like a steadfast tower that never wags
> Its top for all the blowing of the winds;
> For evermore the man in whom is springing
> Thought upon thought, removes from him the mark,
> Because the force of one the other weakens.'"[2]

The meeting with Sordello, who "eyed them after the manner of a couchant lion,"[3] and the magnificent diatribe on Italy, with the appeal to German Albert—
> "Come and behold thy Rome, that is lamenting,
> Widowed, alone, and day and night exclaims,
> 'My Cæsar, why hast thou forsaken me?'"[4]

---

[1] Purg. iv. 88.   [2] Purg. v. 7-18.
[3] Purg. vi. 66.   [4] Purg. vi. 112.

62 DANTE FOR THE GENERAL.

The lap on the hillside where—

"Gold and fine silver, and scarlet, and pearl white,
　The Indian wood resplendent and serene,
　Fresh emerald the moment it is broken.
By herbage and by flowers within that hollow
　Planted, each one in colour would be vanquished,
　As by its greater vanquished is the less."[1]

The oft-quoted opening of Canto viii., which can no more be hackneyed out of its charm than the sunset itself because we see it every day—

"'Twas now the hour that turneth back desire
　In those who sail the sea, and melts the heart,
　The day they've said to their sweet friends farewell,
And the new pilgrim penetrates with love
　If he doth hear from far away a bell
　That seemeth to deplore the dying day."

Or the other almost equally well-known lines on the daybreak—

"Just at the hour when her sad lay begins
　The little swallow, near unto the morning,
　Perchance in memory of her former woes,
And when the mind of man, a wanderer
　More from the flesh, and less by thought imprisoned,
　Almost prophetic in its visions is."[2]

The description of desolation—

[1] Purg. vii. 73.　　　[2] Purg. ix. 13.

> "We stopped upon a plain
> More desolate than roads across the deserts."[1]

The marvellously realistic account of the sculptures on the marble rocks where "Nature's self had there been put to shame;" and that line which must go to the heart of all true artists—

> "In sooth I had not been so courteous
> While I was living, *for the great desire
> Of excellence, on which my heart was bent.*"[2]

Marco Lombardo's fine discourse; Pope Adrian V. and Hugh Capet on avarice; the meeting with Statius, and his philosophic conception of the evolution of Christianity—

> "*Already was the world in every part
> Pregnant with the new creed.*"[3]

The exquisite ending of Canto xxiv.—

> "And as, the harbinger of early dawn,
> The air of May doth move and breathe out fragrance,
> Impregnate all with herbage and with flowers."

The description of the goats in the mid-day heat; and of sleep—

> "Sleep seized upon me—sleep that oftentimes
> Before a deed is done has tidings of it."[4]

---

[1] Purg. x. 20.
[2] Purg. xi. 85.
[3] Purg. xxii. 76.
[4] Purg. xxvii. 92.

Virgil's address to Dante, where we feel that the higher spirit's triumph is assured—

"And said: The temporal fire and the eternal,
    Son, thou hast seen, and to a place art come
    Where of myself no farther I discern.
By intellect and art I here have brought thee;
    Take thine own pleasure for thy guide henceforth;
    Beyond the steep ways and the narrow art thou.
Behold the sun, that shines upon thy forehead;
    Behold the grass, the flowerets, and the shrubs,
    Which of itself alone this land produces.
Until rejoicing come the beauteous eyes
    Which weeping caused me to come unto thee,
    Thou canst sit down, and thou canst walk among them.
Expect no more or word or sign from me;
    Free and upright and sound is thy free will,
    And error were it not to do its bidding;
Thee o'er thyself I therefore crown and mitre!"[1]

And thence to the end of the canticle the beauties are like the March primroses in Sussex lanes—too profuse in their luxuriance for gathering—the air is all impregnate with them.

There are single lines better than any volume of sermons—

    "Pensa che questo dì mai non raggiorna."

    "Think that this day will never dawn again."[2]

"Think that this day will never re-day itself."

[1] Purg. xxvii. 127.   [2] Purg. xii. 84.

Not only that the sweet air which by the sun is gladdened to-day has passed away for ever, but that we too may have passed by on the other side, unheeding the sorrow we might have lightened, the joy we might have welcomed, the love we might have strengthened, the pain we might have lessened. Have we added to some one's good to-day? have we not added to some one's harm? Each day is a renewal of our chance while we live, until the day comes when there is no renewal. It is not a gospel of despair, but a gospel of effort. And this is a single line which, whatever men's differing religious professions may be, the whole human race can go on repeating till the end of time as one of the ultimate expressions of life—

"Pensa che questo dì mai non raggiorna."

DANTE AND THE "NEW REFORMATION."[1]

WHEN we remember that for centuries Catholics tortured Protestants, and that in their turn Protestants tortured Catholics, in the sacred name of religion—a religion, too, supposed to be founded on Divine love—and that they are still ready to rend one another, metaphorically speaking (and to join together in rending "the infidels"), on account of their religious beliefs, it is really very curious and encouraging to find that they can nevertheless lie down amicably together, like the lion and the lamb, in the presence of Dante, the religious poet, notwithstanding that the framework of his great poem is compacted of the very elements that elsewhere have made the two sects

[1] Nineteenth Century, February 1890.

irreconcilable. Each sect seems to find in him its special interpreter. Naturally they have a good deal of quiet mutual contempt for each other's interpretations of the interpreter; but, on the whole, they disagree not more unamiably than other literary disputants, and there are no threats of eternal damnation for any heresies. The Positivists and Agnostics have also taken the pre-eminent poet as their prophet, so that to-day he may be said to focus all the conflicting rays of religious thought in the Western world.

Nothing would probably have surprised the poet himself so much as the idea that he might one day prove to be the missing link between belief, resting on theological dogmas, and a coherent social faith—a social faith dependent on the whole range of the past and looking to the future with unstinted hope, tempered by a great awe of the Eternal and of the everlasting reign of Laws, whereof Science is the handmaiden, and not necessarily divorced from a deep mystical tendency, for it will be nourished by the Bible and by all poetry of a high seriousness, as Mr Matthew Arnold has pointed out.

The situation is not only curious, it is suggestive of possibilities. For there is no more noteworthy phenomenon amongst the forces that are at work moulding the thought of our time, than the extraordinary increase in Dante's influence during the last forty years —especially in England and America. It will probably be well within the mark to say that there are hundreds of readers of the 'Divina Commedia' to-day for every single reader that there was when Dean Church published his well-known scholarly essay in 1850. And this increase has taken place, be it remembered, precisely in the period during which the respect for theological—or ecclesiastical—dogmas has been most rapidly decaying, when it might naturally have been expected that the poem would have lost much of its constraining power over the minds and consciences of its readers, owing to the fact that the vast majority of them have ceased to believe in the corporeal realities of Hell, Purgatory, and Paradise. How, then, is the increase to be accounted for? No doubt it is to some extent due to the cheap editions of Longfellow's translation, for the readers of to-day are not confined to the small circle of Italian scholars. They form a wide public. Then it is a religious book which stands on its intrinsic merits, as the Bible perhaps may some day stand. Every one is permitted to put his own interpretation on the whole scheme and on every incident in it—to adapt its teachings to his own personal idiosyncrasy—and to believe only that which seems to him reasonable to believe. Whatever creeds a man may be brought to recite, he will never practically believe more than that; but the possibilities of belief will, of course, vary, as human minds vary,—that which appears perfectly reasonable to one person often appearing in the highest degree unreasonable to another. What all sects claim, in reading Dante, is untrammelled freedom of the reason as well as of the imagination. Hence the interpretations are as numerous as the readers—but no reader goes empty away. There is matter for all.

It is true that Dante was professedly a great theologian—but he was something more. He was above all things an epoch-making poet, who "carried a light behind"; and he is the true prophet of the New Reformation, because he shows us how a revelation is made, and why it is made. In the 'Comedy' we not only see the effect produced, but we are taken behind the scenes, so to speak, and are shown the means by which it is produced. The pulleys and the properties are all laid bare. The poet has triumphed by the unique power of convincing mankind that a mortal, sufficiently moved by his theme, can by mere force of genius arrogate to himself, and can have accorded to him, the attributes of the Deity. He felt, as all the prophets from Moses onwards had felt before him, that the way to penetrate and enthral the hearts and consciences of his hearers was to bring them a special message direct from the Eternal. It was a device—"une pensée de la jeunesse exécutée dans l'âge mûr;" and in Dante's case it is open to us to accept the message with the consciousness of the device — a device which was worthy of his genius, and his genius was equal to it.

No such superbly audacious undertaking had ever been attempted before. Not that the idea was new—no world-famous idea is, every matured conception being the result of a long process of development; but the method of its application was new. Other prophets, seers, and poets, before and since, have visited in imagination the kingdoms of the dead; but the great Florentine was the first, and will probably be the last, to undertake the delivery of what are supposed to be the everlasting judgments of a personal God, not only on mankind in general, nor only on the great historical characters of the past, but on named individuals contemporary with his own life—on his personal enemies as well as on his personal friends, on the living as well as on the dead. He was the first, and the last, to describe the spirits of the departed as engaged not only in suffering torments or singing hallelujahs, but apparently as still more deeply interested in the political and social questions of the day in Florence, and not unmindful of the personal fortunes and character of the poet Dante nor of their own literary productions. Brunetto Latini, in taking farewell of Dante in hell, touchingly says, "Commended unto thee be my 'Tesoro,' in which I still live, and no more I ask." The great desire of all the spirits is to have their fame re-established in the world, quite oblivious of the practical inconsistency, from the theological point of view, of the same man describing their tortures in hell and at the same time setting them right with mankind. Bocca degli Abati is the only one who sees this logical difficulty, and acknowledges that the less that may be said of him the better it will be. But these are details. The plan of the 'Comedy' results in a bold—perhaps an unconsciously bold—attempt to show that when the assumed divine voice speaks in the language of men, it is in reality the exalted human voice.[1] As one of the most exalted of these voices has said, in language that will endure as long as the human race endures, "*The heavens* declare the glory of God, and *the firmament* showeth His handiwork." The only atheist, or infidel, is the man whose soul is dead to that declaration, which contrasts the infinite greatness of the Eternal with the infinite littleness of man; and it is

---

[1] "The Scripture condescends unto your faculties, and feet and hands to God attributes, and means something else."— Par. iv. 43.

the function of all poets of a high seriousness to act as interpreters between the Eternal and mankind.

And now let the orthodox Protestant Dean of St Paul's tell us how Dante's attempt has succeeded. Writing of the 'Comedy,' he uses these phrases: "It is at once the mirror to all time of the sins and perfections of men, of the judgment and grace of God. . . . History is indeed viewed, not in its ephemeral look, but under the light of God's final judgments, . . . and that which Dante held up before men's awakened and captivated minds was the verity of God's moral government."

What more can be said for prophet or apostle? But no one now asserts that the 'Comedy' is directly inspired—of divine origin —in the sense that such claim is asserted for the Scriptures. What, then, is the exact meaning of Dean Church's words? The answer surely is, that when we analyse what is here meant by the judgment and grace of God, we shall find that it resolves itself into a specially enlightened and elevated human judgment and grace. In fact, it is neither more nor less than the judgment and grace of the man Dante. No doubt every Agnostic would be as ready as Dean Church to attribute an exceptional spiritual power to Dante—as well as to Moses, Ezekiel, and St John. The Agnostic probably would say that the only difference among them is one of degree, not of kind; and it is difficult to understand, from the language quoted above, what further difference the Dean sees. Now if the difference between the inspiration of the Scriptures and the inspiration of a work of human genius like the 'Divine Comedy' can be narrowed down to a difference of degree, the path of the New Reformation will be made easier. For the object to be gained is the liberty of interpreting the Bible with the same freedom as the 'Comedy' may be interpreted — each reader believing in that part of it which is conformable with his reason, and with the best thought and with the social sanctions of the time. No ordinary reader of the 'Comedy' considers himself to be bound by any particular judgment of Dante's which may seem to him to be contrary to that thought and to those sanctions. It is otherwise with the Dantologist, as it is with the

Theologist. Dean Church, for instance, says that "he who could tell her story bowed to the eternal law, and dared not save Francesca." Why, then, it may be asked, did he dare to save Cunizza? The historical evidence (such as it is) does not seem to disclose much difference between the virtues of the two ladies, and if there be any, it is in favour of Francesca. Cunizza could scarcely have said, " Questi, che mai da me non fia diviso : " she would have had to use the plural—" Che forse parrìa forte al vostro vulgo."[1] That which was eternal law in the one case ought certainly to remain eternal in the other. But Dante consigns the one to eternal torment (and, oddly enough, she is the only Christian woman in his hell), and the other to eternal beatitude, because — it happens to suit his dramatic purposes. Again, why should the great spirit of Virgil be left in limbo, "where, without hope, he lives on in desire," whilst the Trojan Ripheus is relegated to an honoured place in paradise, although neither of them had the benefit of that baptism "which is the portal of the faith we hold"?

[1] Par. ix. 36.

The truth is, that it is impossible for us to take these judgments literally. We must always bear in mind that the 'Comedy' is a fourteenth-century drama, and in the nineteenth century it requires to be translated into our language, just as the miraculous portions of the Bible require to be translated. For example, the damnation of Boniface VIII. may have been necessary or expedient as a dramatic incident, whether considered from Dante's personal or from his political point of view; but how can we think of it seriously as God's final judgment? The words are easily written, but the idea is difficult to seize. For is not God—the God of battles—liable to be appealed to by both sides in a conflict? Boniface would, without doubt, and with great show of reason from his point of view, have made an earnest appeal to his God against the gross impiety of the whole conception and execution of the 'Comedy'— against the revolutionary audacity of the layman who had dared to usurp the Papal prerogative and to lock and unlock at his own will the gates of hell, purgatory, and paradise—even in a vision. For it is evident that the vision of a man of genius is capable of being regarded as "history viewed, not in its ephemeral look, but under the light of God's final judgments."

It remains, indeed, a great puzzle for the lay mind to understand how stringent Churchmen are not more affected, and afflicted, by the savour of sacrilege in Dante's whole treatment of his theme. There is, in truth, no escape from a logical *impasse*. If the 'Comedy' is to be regarded in the same light as any other human drama (say "Hamlet," "Lear," or "Faust"), it is undoubtedly a very ruthless satire on the pretensions of the Popes and the Church, showing their insignificance as compared with the pretensions of the poet. If, on the other hand, it is to be regarded as something more than human (and there is evidence that Dante wished it to be so regarded,[1] and many have so regarded it), then we are driven to admit an authority infinitely more binding than any that the Church can lay claim to, because the message from the heavenly powers conveyed by him is more specific, more circumstantial, and more personal than

[1] Par. x. 27, and xxv. 1.

any previous message, whether by the mouth of Moses, Ezekiel, or St John. The Church must make up its mind which horn of the dilemma to choose. If the one, we are not surprised that, within twenty years of his death, the poet's ashes had a very narrow escape of being exhumed and scattered to the winds as those of a heretic; if the other, the marvel is that his revelation is not accepted as the most directly divine message ever delivered, and that St Dante does not take his place as at least the equal of St John, St Peter, or St Paul.

M. Ozanam, the orthodox Catholic Dantologist, is amusing in his way of dealing with the difficulty. "Si Dante *apprécia mal* la piété de St Célestine, le zèle impétueux de Boniface VIII., la science de Jean XXII., ce fut imprudence et colère, ce fut erreur et faute et non pas hérésie." There is a quaint humour in the phrase "*apprécia mal*" when we bear in mind the virulent language in which the misdoings of these Popes are recorded, and that two of them are chiefly known to popular fame outside the Catholic world by Dante's damnation of them. Then there is poor Pope Anastasius also in hell, "whom out of the right way Photinus drew"; but Dr Döllinger assures us that Anastasius was guiltless of any lapse from the true faith. What a reflection it is on theological pretensions when a Pope can be eternally damned by one eminent theologian and certified as sound by another! It would be ludicrous if it were not so serious. The fact is, that a Pope with whom he did not agree seems to have been to Dante like a red flag to a bull. He has placed three of them irredeemably in hell, and Clement V. is relegated to the same hot place (*pozzetto*), where Nicholas III. is waiting for Boniface; whilst Adrian V. is expiating the sin of avarice in purgatory, Martin IV. is expiating the sin of gluttony, and there is not a single Pope in paradise except Gregory the Great, who is set right by Dante on a point of doctrine.[1] Now, whatever may have been the faults and failings of these Popes in life, they all died in the bosom of the Church, repenting of their sins, receiving absolution and extreme unction; and one would have thought that no deadlier blow could be struck

[1] Par. xxviii. 133.

at the authority of the Church than the doffing aside of all these solemn rites and mysteries on the independent judgment of a lay poet. And the same argument may be applied to the admission of the excommunicated Manfred and the pagan Cato to purgatory, as well as of Ripheus to paradise. Which are we to take as God's final judgment, Dante's or the Church's, when Dante damns and the Church canonises? The difficulty can only be solved by the old device of reading with one eye open and the other shut: and so I suppose the Churchmen manage to solve it.

General readers, however, happily for themselves and for their appreciation of everything best worth appreciating in the poem, need not be troubled with these difficulties; for they may believe Dante to have been a man of transcendent genius, with a mighty message to deliver to the world in the early years of the fourteenth century, who used the device of a vision of the unseen as the most powerful vehicle for delivering that message. It would have been impossible for him to have struck so hard or so deep without the intervention of supernatural agency, for the age was one which cast every serious thought into a religious mould—the age following St Louis, when the last crusade had just been accomplished, when miracles were of daily occurrence, when the end of the world was still looked for as imminent, and when hell, purgatory, and paradise were realities such as can scarcely be conceived of by the men of to-day.

But although it was an age that, after the lapse of six centuries, we have the proud privilege of characterising as grossly superstitious (what age is not to the age six hundred years later?), it was also one of the most interesting epochs in the world's history—an epoch vibrating with new life, intellectual, political, religious, and artistic. After the long sleep of over a thousand years, the laity were beginning to recover their freedom of thought. The lawyers were everywhere pitting themselves against the clergy. The two great institutions that had between them governed the Western world for centuries (the Holy Roman Empire and the Holy Roman Church) were grappling in death-throes. The spirit of nationality was crystallising in France and in England, and the bases of representative and constitutional government were being laid, the very forms of which still endure in England to this day. Dante, not knowing, stood at the fountain-head of this stream, which, issuing through the Reformation in Germany, Holland, and England, and the Revolution in France, broadened out into the wide river of American Independence, opening a new industrial era of great hope to mankind. In the intellectual world Roger Bacon[1] had already laid the foundation for his great namesake's superstructure, and had driven the first nails into the coffin of theological dogmas.

Upon this surging "sea of being" was launched the 'Comedy'—like the ark upon the waters after the Deluge—and an appreciative re-born world instinctively and gratefully christened it Divine. It is still divine in the New Reformation's sense of the term, for it is the divine-human. All future ages will pay due tribute to the genius with which the poet worked out his conception; but we shall never

[1] It is noteworthy that Dante never mentions Roger Bacon's name.

form a just idea of the man Dante unless we recognise that he had his full share of human errors and weaknesses, even as the reputed author of the Psalms had his. The one was an impassioned Italian poet and prophet (and it needs an Italian to comprehend his nature as well as his intellect), the other was an impassioned Hebrew prophet and poet; and both of them had the defects of their qualities—defects which must never be forgotten. They were merciless and unforgiving to their enemies, capable of any injustice where their own egoistic preferences were crossed;[1] but whether by reason of, or in despite of, their defects of character, they both knew how to sound the depths of the human heart, its capabilities for good and evil, its great yearnings. They were both men of sorrows and acquainted with sin, and consequently they were able to let shafts of light down into

---

[1] Note especially the case of Guido da Montefeltro—the "romanzo storico" of "the promise long and the fulfilment short." On the face of it, it is ridiculous to suppose that Boniface—who is described by Dante as a fox, and was undoubtedly a very accomplished Italian intriguer—would seek for such ingenuous and childlike advice. It is said that the story is not mentioned by any contemporary.

the secret places of men's souls. And this is the characteristic attribute of the great seer, whether he be a Hebrew prophet, a Greek tragedian, a Roman poet, a Christian apostle, or a Dante. He must have the eye to penetrate the eternal truths of life, and the real motives which actuate human conduct—to see things as they are, disengaged from the conventional point of view of the day. The motto of the 'Comedy' might be taken from St Francis: "What every man is in the eyes of God, that he is and no more." The God within each man knows what that is.

> "How many are esteemed great kings up there
> Who here shall be like unto swine in mire,
> Leaving behind them horrible dispraises." [1]

> "But look thou, many crying are, Christ! Christ!
> Who at the judgment shall be far less near
> To Him than some shall be who knew not Christ.
> Such Christians shall the Ethiop condemn,
> When the two companies shall be divided,
> The one for ever rich, the other poor.
> What to *your* kings may not the Persians say,
> When they that volume opened shall behold
> In which are written down all their dispraises?" [2]

---

[1] Inf. viii. 49.   [2] Par. xix. 106.

"Let not Dame Bertha nor Ser Martin think,
 Seeing one steal, another offering make,
 To see them in the arbitrament divine,
 For one may rise, and fall the other may."[1]

Dante's undying influence with the great mass of lay-readers is due to this penetrating power of seeing things as they are, and making us see ourselves as we are, unmasking the shams of the world, and passing beyond the pretensions of the Church to absolve and remit sins. He knew that wrong-doing and its punishment are as inseparable as the root and the flower of a poisonous plant, and that if the mills of the gods grind slow they grind exceeding fine.[2] Then his clear perception of the necessity for social regeneration appeals directly to the modern spirit. Looking round on the world from his standpoint as an exile and a wanderer deprived of all worldly goods, he vividly realised the misery wrought by the excessive claims of individual selfishness—the envy, the arrogance, the sloth, and the avarice—and he conceived his vision as the strongest possible appeal to men's fears and to their hopes.

[1] Par. xiii. 142.   [2] Cf. Par. xxii. 16.

The fundamental idea of the 'Comedy,' as of the Bible, consists in the precept, "Love thy neighbour as thyself."[1] As Beatrice beautifully puts it—

> "Of those things only should one be afraid
> Which have the power of doing others harm.
> Of the rest no; because they are not fearful."[2]

It is an essentially social basis. The application of the idea to life will enlarge with the developing conscience of mankind. At one time it will require the support of a supernatural sanction, at another time it will rest on the social sanction; but it will ever remain the basis of all true religion—of universal religion

---

[1] "Love must be the seed within yourselves of every virtue and every act that merits punishment."—Purg. xvii. 103.

> " Hence if, discriminating, I judge well,
> The *evil* that one loves is of one's neighbour,
> And this is born in three modes in your clay.
> There are, who, by *abasement of their neighbour*,
> Hope to excel, and therefore only long
> That from his greatness he may be cast down;
> There are, who power, grace, honour, and renown
> Fear they may *lose because another rises*,
> Thence are so sad that *the reverse* they love;
> And there are those whom *injury* seems to chafe,
> So that it makes them *greedy for revenge*,
> And such must needs shape out *another's* harm.
> This threefold love is wept for down below."
> —Purg. xvii. 112.

[2] Inf. ii. 88.

—because it demonstrably leads to the kingdom of heaven. If we could conceive of a world where the doctrine was not only preached but practised, we could conceive of a world without sin. For all sin or wrong-doing is finally referable to the love of self, instead of love of others; and the love of others is the love of God, for "God is love."[1] In these three words of St John lie the foundation and the reconciliation of all religions.

We have only to read the literature of the opposing Christian sects in order to acknowledge that we are still a long way off this final stadium of development; but the worship of human goodness (which is the highest goodness we know from experience) is one form of worshipping God, and our best image of God's love is the love of the mother for her child, of the child for its mother. All readers of Dante know that when he wishes to strike his tenderest chord, this love is the note he touches.[2] And in another art—in the Madonna di San Sisto, the ideal mother with the ideal Child

---

[1] Cf. Inf. i. 39; and Par. xxxiii. 145.
[2] Inf. xxiii. 38; Purg. xxx. 44; Par. i. 101, xiv. 64, xxii. 1, xxiii. 121, xxx. 82.

in her arms — we recognise the everlasting emblem of the religion of Christianity, of the religion of humanity, and haply also of their junction.

Hell can never be reached except when the love of others is dead within us, whether we regard hell as an actual place of torment or as a subjective mental and moral state. So long as there is love of others in the heart there is hope, and that is the secret of Jesus. He is the true corner-stone, for our finest conceptions of perfect love cluster round His personality, real or ideal. The authenticity of the Gospel narratives may be proved or disproved, but the character of Jesus as it has formed itself for us during nineteen centuries will remain as a type. It is true that in Dante's poem the finest essence of Christ's teaching and example is often overlaid by the requirements of the system of the Roman Church, and by the poet's own passionate unforgiving nature; but no one has shown more clearly than Dante how treachery, fraud, covetousness, pride, anger, sloth, and all other deadly sins, have their common root in love of self, causing us to claim more than our fair share. What we have to aim at is "hungering at all times so far as is just."[1] In a few striking lines he puts his finger on the diseased spot in our social structure :—

> "O human race! why dost thou set thy heart
> Where interdict of partnership must be?[2]
> . . . . . .
> 'What did the spirit of Romagna mean,
> Mentioning interdict and partnership?'
> Whence he[3] to me: 'Of his own greatest failing
> He knows the harm; and therefore wonder not
> If he reprove us, that we less may rue it.
> *Because are thither pointed your desires*
> *Where by companionship each share is lessened,*
> *Envy doth ply the bellows to your sighs.*
> But if the love of the supernal sphere
> Should *upwardly* direct your aspiration,
> There would not be that *fear* within your breast;
> For there, as much the more as one says *Our*,
> So much the more of good each one possesses,
> And more of charity in that cloister burns.'"[4]

The purchase which capital has acquired over the products of labour is seen to be the root of some of the greatest evils from which humanity suffers. In the very opening of the poem Avarice is figured as a she-wolf

[1] Purg. xxiv. 154; and cf. Par. vii. 25.
[2] Purg. xiv. 86.   [3] Virgil.   [4] Purg. xv. 45.

> "that with all hungerings
> Seemed to be laden in her meagreness,
> And many folk has caused to live forlorn!"[1]

She is to be driven back to hell, "there from whence Envy first did let her loose." The application is much wider than to the mere avarice of the clergy. The sudden gains are set down as the ruin of Florence. Plutus is referred to as the great enemy, and Virgil is constantly reminding Dante of the dangers arising from "the accursed hunger of gold"; particularly in the beautiful lines :—

> "For all the gold that is beneath the moon
> Or ever has been, of these weary souls
> Could never make a single one repose."[2]

Beatrice, at the beginning of that charming passage in the "Paradise" where she anticipates much that Wordsworth has said as to "the youth who daily farther from the East must travel," says :—

> "O Covetousness, that mortals dost ingulf
> Beneath thee so, that no one hath the power
> Of drawing back his eyes from out thy waves!"[3]

Dante himself, too, takes occasion to blow the

---

[1] Inf. i. 49; cf. Purg. xx. 10. [2] Inf. vii. 64.
[3] Par. xxvii. 121, and cf. xxx. 139.

bellows on the flames that are licking the soles of Pope Nicholas the Third, by reminding him how "his avarice afflicts the world—trampling the good and lifting the depraved"; and the following lines put into the mouth of Hugh Capet have still their pointed significance in our own Vanity Fair. They refer to Charles the Second of Apulia, who married his daughter to Azzo the Third da Este of Ferrara.

> "The other, now gone forth, ta'en in his ship,
>   See I his daughter sell, and chaffer for her
>   As corsairs do with other female slaves.
> What more, O Avarice, canst thou do to us,
>   Since thou my blood so to thyself hast drawn,
>   It careth not for its own proper flesh?"[1]

These are only a few passages, that can be multiplied over and over again, showing that social questions form the very warp and woof of the 'Comedy.' The poet is in truth much more concerned with the affairs of this world than with the next—although the scene is laid in the latter. He is not afraid to use the lash, and it falls on peculiarly tender places in the modern conscience. He saw clearly that the voluntary poverty of the Friars was

[1] Purg. xx. 79.

the most helpful gift that the medieval Church had given to the world[1] (our Bishops and Deans must have their withers wrung as well as the rest of us); and as he had himself been involuntarily stripped of all his own worldly goods, he was in a position to recognise the fact that the ever-increasing inequality in the distribution of wealth is the greatest danger to social wellbeing. The fierce white light that he throws on the danger of the two excesses, in acquiring individual wealth and in profusely spending it, illumines for us the higher aspirations of the true spirit of social regeneration—that spirit which is looming up so largely through the world to-day. Not the crude spirit which would risk reducing order to chaos by violent methods, but the spirit which is at work modifying and changing our ideal of possession from an individual to a social basis. Dante sombrely shadows forth the outlines of the mighty problem, and to the modern mind it is one of the most interesting of all the interesting elements in the 'Comedy.'

[1] St Francis, Par. xi. 64-67 *et seq.;* St Dominic, Par. xii. 82 *et seq.;* and cf. Par. xxii. 82.

His descriptions of the spirit-world may be taken as figures, symbols, types. No doubt many people will maintain that if you take away the belief in the future life as represented in the 'Comedy,' you take away all meaning from the poem, which may be compared to saying that if you take away the Jewish ordinances from the Old Testament you take away its essential part. Those ordinances had no doubt a deep and important significance to the Israelites; their significance has ceased for us, but the vital teaching of the Old Testament is not in the least dependent on them. It is as true to us as the day it was written, because it is the highest poetry. I suppose in Dante's time there were believers in the future life as described by him; but does any one believe in it literally to-day? Did he believe in it himself? It is much more difficult to think that he did, than to think that he did not. It is hard for us to imagine that the torments were really such, and felt by the shades to be such, as they are described when we find Farinata in hell saying to Dante, in reference to the banishment of the Ghibellines by the poet's ancestors, and in reply to a taunt that they had not "acquired the art" of returning from their banishment to Florence—

"And if they have *not* learned that art aright,
That more tormenteth me than doth this bed."[1]

It certainly puts a different complexion on these torments when we are told that a sufferer feels them less than the thought that his descendants had not found the way of reinstating themselves in power in the city of Florence, and that he "held hell in great despite." Again, if Dante had believed in the actuality of his own hell, he would scarcely have made Virgil say to Capaneus—

"O Capaneus, in that is not extinguished
Thine arrogance, thou punished art the more:
*Not any torment saving thine own rage
Would be unto thy fury pain complete.*"[2]

Nor, on the other hand, if he had believed in the reality of his own paradise, can we imagine him introducing his pride of birth in meeting his great ancestor Cacciaguida; nor, when he has been brought face to face with the Virgin Mary, the Angel Gabriel, St John,

[1] Inf. x. 76.   [2] Inf. xiv. 63.

and Moses, allowing St Bernard to finish his introduction with such lines as these:—

> "But since the moments of thy vision fly,
> Here will we make full stop, *as a good tailor
> Who makes the gown according to his cloth.*"[1]

Undoubtedly one of the most puzzling among the many puzzling problems coiled in the mysterious verses of the 'Comedy' is to conceive how we are meant to take this future life. There are so many curious incongruities in the treatment of it, that we are sometimes driven to think that

> "Perhaps his doctrine is of other guise
> Than the words sound, and possibly may be
> With meaning that is not to be derided."[2]

In the verses spoken by Cacciaguida we find a suggestion that may be taken as a reference to subjective immortality:—

> "Because thy life into the future reaches
> Beyond the punishment of their perfidies."[3]

To which Dante replies:—

[1] Par. xxxii. 139. [2] Par. iv. 55
[3] Par. xvii. 98.

"And if I am a timid friend to truth,
*I fear lest I may lose my life with those
Who will hereafter call this time the olden.*"[1]

He conjures the spirits in hell :—

"So may your memory not steal away
In the first world from out the minds of men,
But so may it survive 'neath many suns."[2]

And Cunizza says that of Folco the troubadour :—

"Great fame remained; and ere it die away
This hundredth year shall yet quintupled be.
*See if man ought to make him excellent,
So that another life the first may leave.*"[3]

This is probably the immortality that Dante refers to when he says to Brunetto Latini, "You taught me how a man becomes eternal."[4] Of course, there are scores of passages in the 'Convito' as well as in the 'Comedy' which can be adduced in proof of Dante's complete belief in the accepted view of his century on this subject, just as an equal number of passages can be adduced in proof of his complete belief in the accepted view of his century as to the divine appointment

[1] Par. xvii. 118.   [2] Inf. xxix. 103.
[3] Par. ix. 39.   [4] Inf. xv. 85.

of the holy Roman emperors. All we can with certainty affirm is, that whatever interpretations may be put on the poet's descriptions of the future life, these descriptions have no warrant from Scriptural authority, but rest entirely on the authority of his own imagination. In that great subtle mind there was room for many conceptions of immortality, and for many motives in favour of enforcing a particular conception. No one knew better than he that human nature is so constituted that the reiterated assertion by a supreme artist of a claim to superhuman knowledge, and experience beyond the grave, although admittedly in a vision, compels an attention and a belief that would never be accorded to any mortal who had cast his ideas into a different form.

And no writer ever made such personal claims for himself. He tells us at once of his beautiful style that has done honour to him, and how the five poets whom he regarded as the greatest of antiquity made him the sixth in their own band. Brunetto Latini prophesies smooth things to him, and says he is "the sweet fig amongst the crabbed sorbs." Guido del Duca, Judge Nino, Currado Malaspina, Sapìa, Marco Lombardo, Hugh Capet, Guido Guinicelli, Cacciaguida, Charles Martel, Thomas Aquinas, Justinian, and indeed most of the shades of the departed, assure him that he is particularly beloved of God —an assurance that was scarcely required, as the very fact of his journey was sufficient evidence of his "especial grace." He addresses the Gemini, "O glorious stars, O light impregnated with mighty virtue, from which I acknowledge all of my genius, whatsoe'er it be."[1] In paradise St Peter himself encircles Dante's brow after his examination on faith — a much greater honour for the poet than "taking the laurel crown at his baptismal font." St James expresses his gratitude to the expert disciple who shows such proficiency in the doctrine of hope, St John catechises him on Divine Love, and St Bernard introduces him to the Virgin Mary. He receives direct from the mouths of these saints elucidations of various disputed points of doctrine,[2] and is commanded to tell the blind world how it is going wrong by

[1] Par. xxii. 112.   [2] Par. xxix. 70 *et seq.*

not separating the Spiritual and the Temporal powers. Much as we may bow to Dante's genius to-day, it is utterly impossible for us by any effort of the imagination to realise the impression that these intimate relations with the saints in paradise must have produced on the religious minds of the time in Florence. To think that their own fellow-citizen could say at the sight of the blessed Rose:—

> "I who to the divine had from the human,
> From time into eternity had come,
> From Florence to a people just and sane,
> With what amazement must I have been filled!"[1]

A selection from the various writers on the 'Divina Commedia' and their various interpretations will convince us of the impossibility of defining Dante's own inmost beliefs. Probably no other human soul ever believed exactly as he believed. Probably no two human souls from the beginning of time have ever believed exactly alike as to the eternities —a thought which ought to make us charitable in our judgment of each other's beliefs.

[1] Par. xxxi. 37.

But we may observe that whenever he comes out of the region of barren metaphysics into his own region of exquisite poetical images, we can all go along with him. No one of a religious mind, whatever may be his creed, can fail to appreciate such lines as these:—

> "Into the justice sempiternal
> The power of vision that your world receives
> As eye into the ocean penetrates;
> Which, though it see the bottom near the shore,
> Upon the deep perceives it not, and yet
> 'Tis there, but it is hidden by the depth."[1]

This is the very gospel of Agnosticism. It is true that in another passage he tells us, "If so the Scriptures were not over you for doubting there were marvellous occasion;" but then it is precisely on the interpretation of these Scriptures that the whole difference between Catholics and Protestants has turned. Certainly Dante's literal interpretation will not coincide with the Protestant's interpretation, still less with the Unitarian's, and least of all with the Agnostic's, but they all join in admiration of the beauty of his imagery:—

[1] Par. xix. 58.

"Within the deep and luminous subsistence
   Of the high light appeared to me three circles
   Of threefold colours and of one dimension,
And in the second seemed the first reflected
   As Iris is by Iris, and the third
   Seemed fire that equally from both is breathed." [1]

Mr Lowell takes this as an "image of that Power, Love, and Wisdom, one in essence but trine in manifestation, to answer the needs of our triple nature and satisfy the senses, the heart, and the mind." That is an interpretation to which every one can subscribe. Professor Huxley and Cardinal Manning can meet on it, although it conveys such different conceptions to their two minds. It has been said that Dante "translated into the language of the multitude what the Schools had done to throw light on the deep questions of human existence." [2] But he has done much more. As a great poet he has soared infinitely beyond and above their metaphysics, although it is evident that he judged it to be necessary that the world of his day should be governed by their system, or rather he placed his hopes in the idealisation of the

[1] Par: xxxiii. 115.   [2] Dean Church (Essay on Dante).

two systems then existing—the Holy Roman Church and the Holy Roman Empire. But to make the arrangements completely satisfactory to his critical and exacting mind, he would have required, for their actual working, one Dante as Pope, and another Dante as Emperor. He was keenly alive to the necessity of a divine authority for the Temporal power as well as for the Spiritual power, because he knew that the crowd must have emphatic warrant; and we get some help to understanding his mental attitude towards miracles and revelations from the serious argument in the 'De Monarchiâ,' founding the claims of Rome to the empire of the world on the old Roman miracles—the geese of the Capitol, the hailstorm which checked Hannibal, &c., "proved by the testimony of illustrious authorities." If any one wishes to learn the value of the testimony of illustrious authorities, it is only necessary to look up the records of the Tichborne trial.

Dean Church remarks on Dante's belief in these early miracles that "the intellectual phenomenon is a strange one." Perhaps the stranger one is to accept some miracles and to reject others, when they are all said to be "proved by the testimony of illustrious authorities." Our poet carried his belief backwards from the early Christian miracles, just as Dr Newman carries his belief in them forwards. The logic is unimpeachable. Every phenomenon claiming acceptance as a miracle must be subjected to the same rigorous scientific tests, although I suppose the most sceptical of men admits that all life is one long miracle, from birth to death, in the sense that the first cause is unknown. It may be said that these arguments for the miraculous sanctions of the Roman Empire are in the 'De Monarchiâ,' which was probably written before 1300. But they are not confined to that essay. The belief was a common one at the period, and if we were to take out of the 'Comedy' all the direct and indirect references to the divinity of the Empire, we should have a body of doctrine fully as convincing as the theological dogmas. God is alluded to as the Emperor, the Virgin Mary as Augusta, and in purgatory Beatrice tells Dante that he will only be a short time there, and then will be with her for evermore in paradise, "a citizen of that

Rome where Christ is Roman." Judas, who betrayed Christ, and Brutus and Cassius, who betrayed Cæsar, are all punished together; and the Roman eagle is one of the most conspicuous features in paradise as well as in purgatory. So far as Dante's arguments go, the reasons for believing in the divine origin of the Empire are just as convincing as the reasons for believing in the divine origin of the Church. And in a certain sense we all believe in this kind of divinity. There was a time (not long ago) when this divinity did hedge our kings. It still hedges the English constitution to the Englishman, the American constitution to the American, and so forth: for the frame of civil government is the symbol of the reign of law, which mankind has seen to be necessary for its salvation and endurance. In that sense it is eternal or divine—just as the decisions of a supreme court of appeal are practically infallible. But at the same time we know that if the majority of the men in a country determine to alter them they will be altered, and generally improved. Institutions develop as the race develops. As Dante puts it, "though there are other beings which with him have understanding, yet this understanding is not, as man's, capable of development."[1] "Semper eadem" is an impossible motto in this quickly changing world—quickly changing especially from the point of view of a thousand years being as one day.

Dante shows us the real meaning, to his mind, of the divine origin and the supernatural sanction, when he says: "If the Church had power to bestow authority on the Roman prince, she would have it either from God, or from herself, or from some emperor, or from the universal consent of mankind, *or at least of the majority of mankind.*" This is indeed the *vox populi vox Dei.* It is a firm social basis: for it practically acknowledges the divinity of the State, supported by supernatural sanctions—sanctions which, as Gibbon said of other sanctions, "to the people were equally true, to the philosopher were equally false, and to the magistrate were equally useful." Now, the State can stand unaided on the basis of human reason. No wonder that the 'De Monarchiâ' is in the Index Expurgatorius. For it is certain that one of the institutions

[1] De Monarchiâ.

which Dante believed to be as divinely ordained as the Church has passed away; the other may pass away also; but, because the social instincts of man are ever ripening to a finer fruit, the human race will still go on developing, though, perhaps, under different conceptions of spiritual and temporal direction. Dogmas will alter—as they always have altered—with the process of the suns; but the spirit of truth and justice will remain, because it is "within men, like the kingdom of God, as a great spiritual yearning." We may disbelieve all Dante's supernatural ideas, just as we disbelieve the miraculous sanctions of the Roman Empire, or the Ptolemaic system of astronomy; but they were not "false errors," and he will remain to us as the greatest poet of humanity, because none has seen more clearly the seed of social disease and the need for social regeneration. The germ of the latest political ideal too—the parliament of man, the federation of the world—is to be found in his writings.

And great as his claims may be as a thinker, they are still greater as an artist. Through his dramatic representation he has riveted the attention of mankind on his writing for six centuries, and his influence is as fresh and infinitely wider to-day than it has ever been before. The interest of his poem centres in his own personality. Its origin is constantly attributed to his desire of deifying Beatrice; but if we look at it closely, the result is not the deification of Beatrice, but the deification of Dante. The lady of his mind becomes more and more shadowy, melts into his ideal self, but his own personality becomes ever more sharply defined—cut out in clear relief against the background of the poem—so that at the last we find that Beatrice is not a being apart from him, but that she has become a part of his being, and that she, the angels, the saints, the spirits in torment, and Lucifer, are all used as adjuncts to enable a supreme artist to deliver one of the greatest of human messages to a social world.

As the first Christian prophet who has given us a revelation without the pretension of any miraculous intervention—a revelation which we are not bound to accept by any theological dogma, but the essence of which (its perception of the social bases of human virtues and vices) forces itself on our belief as the truth, whether we like it or not—and as the first great literary artist who has known how to seize the essential in that which he wished to portray, and by a few strong strokes to leave a perfect picture on the mental retina—who has known how to press out the juice of his conception, throwing away the pulp and the rind—in a word, as the first great impressionist, the Italian poet has fixed his place as the guiding star to the modern intellectual movement. And if the Dante dome is wide enough to cover opinions and feelings as antipodal as those of Protestants and Positivists, Roman Catholics and Agnostics, shall the Christian Cathedral of the future offer a less hospitable shelter? Surely there will be room in it for all the men, women, and children who may be seeking in any way to leave this confused world a little better than they found it, whatever may be their beliefs—or no beliefs—in dogmatic theology. The Church speaks brave words as to its increasing influence, but the voice of Rome sounds tremulous. It is too late nowadays to anathematise men of science as infidels. The Church of the future must recruit them to herself as the best soldiers in the ranks of the truly religious. For the pursuit of real science is the pursuit of truth —truth in which alone the intellect finds rest :—

> "Light intellectual replete with love,
> Love of true good replete with ecstasy,
> Ecstasy that transcendeth every sweetness." [1]

This too is religion, and the highest poetry is its best expression.

[1] Par. xxx. 40.

THE NEW WORLD.[1]

WE know how difficult it is to form any true estimate of popular opinion in our own little island, where the area is exceedingly limited, where all shades of opinion are fairly and faithfully represented by an ubiquitous, an independent, and a self-respecting newspaper press mainly intent on recording the facts as they exist, and where, consequently, we have all the appliances for arriving at a reasonable judgment. Yet every general election teaches us how hopelessly even the most knowing ones—the men whose whole function in life is to know—are led astray on great and well-defined issues. We may judge, therefore, how much more difficult it is to

[1] Nineteenth Century, March 1891.

arrive at any accurate knowledge of popular opinion among the English-speaking peoples, amounting to double our own numbers, scattered over the vast area of the New World. We run constant risk of attributing to them imaginary states of feeling begotten of our own sentiment and our own egoistic desires, where our wish is father to our thought. A case in point is the confident notion very generally entertained in this country that there is a strong *popular* feeling in our great colonies in favour of Imperial Federation. Perhaps it is scarcely worth while either to deny or to affirm the existence of this feeling, because the scheme of federation is as yet so formless and so vague—it is still so completely outside the area of practical politics—that no one can possibly have formed an intelligent judgment upon it; but while the project is still in the air it may not be amiss to call attention, in the fewest possible words, to certain general principles which must necessarily underlie it, and which have scarcely yet received all the consideration that they merit. We want fairly to envisage the situation—to face its realities. We are concerned with the growth of a New

World, and we may be sure that it has a natural principle of growth which can only be departed from under pain of retributive penalties. Is this principle of growth the same for Canada and Australia as it is for England? Have we fully considered the question from their point of view? For instance, if we set ourselves to think of the relations between the New World and the Old, what is the first and the most important consideration that arises in our minds? An Englishman, primed by Professor Seeley, will promptly answer, "The expansion of England." But an American will certainly answer, "The predominance of American ideas," and an Australian will probably answer, "Advance Australia!"

Here then, at the outset, we find that the question is not a simple one, as we get these very different answers from the three parties principally interested. The Englishman's answer is obviously too narrow, the American's is perhaps too shallow, and the Australian's is certainly too callow—if the expression may be used in regard to such a rapidly growing young bird. Yet there is some truth in each answer. It may be said that, in a restricted sense, the Englishman's is true of the past, the American's is true of the present, and the Australian's may possibly be true of the future.

But to express the full significance of the New World's development, we must find a formula that will combine the three points of view. Perhaps that formula may be "The expansion of the great humanitarian movement," which is broader than the expansion of England, deeper than the predominance of American ideas, and higher than 'Advance Australia!' For if we go back to the birth of the New World and the tradition which it has created, we can trace its descent directly from that movement—a movement which was, in its origin, coincident with the Reformation, which was nourished by the eighty years' struggle of the Netherlands against Spain, and which afterwards received the most quickening impulse from the French Revolution. The movement was based on revolt against tyranny, privilege, and oppression, in favour of liberty, equality, and fraternity. Its ultimate aim was to abolish monarchy, to abolish aristocracy, to abolish the connection between Church and State, and to establish the sovereignty of the people. It profoundly modified all previously existing ideas of religion and politics, and set in motion the great long wave of emigration which has not only been the overflow of population, but has borne onward in its course a continuous protest against many of the ideas, the sentiments, and the methods (particularly the military methods) of the Old World, and landed on the shores of the New World a people determined to try a wholly new system founded on the basis of industrialism.

And here we get to the very kernel of the question. Industrialism, as opposed to militarism, is now the central idea of the New World—the pivot upon which the New World may be said to turn. Here we find a vital principle—not merely a vague aspiration as it still is in the Old World—and we must lay hold of it as an elementary and fundamental consideration if we are to understand rightly the relations between the two worlds. For the full accomplishment of this stage of social development signalises a new departure of immense historical importance. It changes the whole attitude and the ideals of a people—

whether for better or for worse is a point we need not argue here; there is, no doubt, much to be said on both sides. For it may be admitted that intense industrial competition often produces its own miseries, its own cruelties, its own degradations, its own sacrifices of human life and wellbeing, without the balance of ennobling elements that military undertakings for a great and worthy common end have sometimes, though rarely, called forth. The *change*, however, is the important consideration, and it must never be lost sight of when we attempt to gauge the sentiment and the probable future action of the New World—for change of function leads to change of organism.

What do we mean, for instance, when we speak now of the United States as a dominating power? We mean dominating by *ideas*, not by physical force. They are not an aggressive power (though often a blustering power), but they have been, and are, an incalculably powerful factor in revolutionising the thinking and the feeling of half the world. To the future historian one of the most striking phenomena of the last quarter of this century will be the extraordinary increase that he will discern in the relative *weight* of America during this period compared with former years. He will be called on to chronicle the fact that her example was relied on as an argument in favour of the scheme for British Imperial Federation, and notwithstanding its curious inapplicability, he will find that the analogy was made use of for years after its absurdity had been demonstrated. Imitation is the sincerest form of flattery, and the flattery is none the less sincere even though the successful imitation be impossible.

We all know what the United States of America are. They are equal sovereign states, which have delegated certain powers to a central authority of their own creation, under a rigid written Constitution. They are contiguous to one another, containing some sixty-five million people, with identical language, identical institutions, identical aims, and identical currency; threatened by no strong neighbouring powers; no part of the federation bound by obligations or treaties to which any other part objects, or is ever likely to object; with absolute freedom of trade internally and protection externally—a commercial policy, by the way, which seems to be the present ideal of the whole New World—alas, for the irony of fate! Compact within themselves, and with continuous lines of railroad (about 170,000 miles in all) running through the whole length and breadth of the federation, they form a colossal power, solid by reason of the diffused ownership of the land, the diversity of employment between agriculture and manufactures, the rapidity of inter-communication; and although practically only a hundred years old—not yet older than individuals still living amongst us—they are already in actual wealth the richest community and the greatest manufacturing community in the world, potentially fabulous in population and power, but with no standing army and a comparatively small navy. Yet they are strong for defence, because having no outlying dependencies; and in the last resort, being absolutely independent of external commerce, owing to their capacity for supplying abundantly within their own borders every need of man, all that they require is a navy strong enough for purely defensive purposes. And we, as free-traders, must admit that protection of native industries, notwithstanding all its drawbacks, has given them this incidental advantage of rendering them independent of the outside world in case of war, which is not a negligable quantity even to a New World industrial power "in this so-called nineteenth century." The advantage, however, has been bought at the price of the eclipse—at any rate the temporary eclipse—of their mercantile marine, and that is not the only price they have had to pay, and will have to pay, for protection. . . . "But that is another story."

These states have had the good fortune, through favouring circumstances, to be able to build up for themselves a tradition of peaceable expansion, so that militarism is no longer a factor in the conduct of their affairs, nor in their thinking. The bayonet has been banished as a standing institution, though ready enough to reappear if occasion requires. The civil war which ended in 1865 was caused indirectly, if not directly, by the abnormal institution of slavery, and instead of increasing the tendency towards militarism, it really advanced the cause of industrialism more than any event in history. The whole armed forces on both sides were at once quietly reabsorbed into the industrial population; the great lesson was taught to the world that industrialism does not necessarily lead to national impotence; and the experience gained by the Northerners, of the difficulty of governing an unwilling South after the war, has made them more averse than before to the responsibility of introducing any possibly recalcitrant elements into their commonwealth.

Perhaps four Americans out of five look on it as "manifest destiny" that the whole continent must sooner or later come into their system of federation, but they are content to know that if this result is to be arrived at, it will be by the peaceful power of railroads and commercial intercourse, and not by force of arms. In any previous period of history sixty-five million people wedged in, as the Americans are, between five million Canadians on their northern border and ten million Mexicans on their southern border, would have been restless in their endeavours to subdue at least one of these weaker neighbours; and the war of

1861-65 conclusively proved that they were not prevented by any lack of the fighting and organising qualities that make conquering nations, but rather by the reasoned conviction that aggression and a feverish desire for extension is a mistaken policy in the case of an industrial people already possessed of sufficient territory for its reasonable expansion. Whatever feeling there may have been forty or fifty years ago in favour of forcible annexation, has gradually died out. There is certainly no such feeling to-day; and this national attitude marks an epoch, for it is the practical acknowledgment that the New World is to be unified, not conquered, by the strongest power, and that the only true, enduring, and endurable union is a voluntary one based on community of interests and aims. But the pact once made has to be kept.

Here, then, we have the example of a true federation, the outcome of a natural principle of growth, with nothing forced about it. It is the characteristic product of the century, and carries a world of meaning in its short history, for it has opened a new era to mankind by revolutionising the means for attaining given ends. And this brings us to the probable point of issue between English and American ideas as to the future development of the North American continent. Canada has the proverbial "three courses" open to her. She may (1) determine to maintain existing relations with the mother country, or (2) to set up for herself, or (3) to be absorbed into the American federation. The difficulty in the first case is the natural instinct, rapidly maturing into a passion, for a real national existence independent of leading-strings—a passion which is palpable to every observer in the Dominion, and which can scarcely be gratified except at the expense of a revolution in our English institutions,—a revolution, or an evolution, in the direction of Imperial Federation, for which under existing social conditions we are not yet prepared, and which presents so many practical difficulties that its successful accomplishment within any measurable distance of time is exceedingly doubtful, and time is of the essence of the contract. The difficulty in the second case is the constant impact of 65,000,000 people upon 5,000,000 along an artificial frontier 4000 miles long, the two peoples being really divided by no irreconcilable differences of race and religion, and having, as a matter of fact, every material interest in common; so that, under these circumstances, it would scarcely seem to be worth their while to run the risks of perpetual jealousies and collisions for the sake of a sentiment confined probably to a minority of the whole population on the Canadian side. The difficulty in the third case is precisely this anti-American sentiment among "the classes" in the Dominion—a sentiment in which the French Canadians join, and which is mainly based on a broad and commendable feeling of individuality and distrust in the political purity of American institutions,[1] in addition to the sentiment of nationality and loyalty to the British connection. Turn it which way we will, however, we shall find that, whichever of the three facets

[1] Americans will no doubt be amused by my ingenuous belief in the "purity principles" of the Canadians, after recent revelations. But I leave the sentence as it was written, because it represented a general and a genuine, if a mistaken, conviction among Englishmen up to a year ago (1892).

of the problem fronts us, there is always one thing clear—namely, that by the inexorable logic of facts Canada is essentially a New World industrial power. She is approaching very rapidly to the parting of the ways, and one of the most interesting and far-reaching events of the near future will be the course she decides on as to commercial union with the United States; for it can scarcely be supposed that she will *permanently* cut herself off from the great market at her doors, and commercial union will almost inevitably bring her to a closer bond. No man can tell yet what her decision will be. All that can be certainly affirmed is, that it will be one of the most momentous decisions in the history of the New World; because, if the Dominion and Newfoundland eventually determine to throw in their lots with the United States, the last material link between the Old World and the continents of the Western Hemisphere will be snapped, and the North American continent, under a single federation, will present to view the most solid power that the world has ever seen—purely industrial, armed only for defence, and with no apparent bone of contention between itself and any other power either of the Old or the New World. This solution would not be agreeable to us in England with our present ideas, and all that can be said in its favour from our point of view is that it would minimise the danger of future collisions between the United States and ourselves, and it would have a favourable effect on the whole future progress of industrialism. Again, if we could view the question from a wholly impartial standpoint, it might be said that a diversity of institutions would be a sensible gain in the development of so great a country as the North American continent; but, on the other hand, it must be admitted that the present tendency in human affairs is towards federation—towards unification of contiguous areas, with peoples of the same race, speaking the same language, and having common interests and aims. As the means of communication increase, nationalism becomes a feebler, and internationalism a stronger, motive power; and this is more particularly the case in the New World. This tendency is much the most important and the most interesting feature in the world's politics to-day; and if the federation of the North American continent ever takes place, it will probably exercise a decisive influence in moulding the destinies of Australia.

The United States of Australasia are still in the embryonic stage, and the cry of "Advance Australia!" is perhaps premature as the watchword of the New World; but they are, nevertheless, distinctly leading the way in attempting solutions of many social problems, with more or less success. Any one who has been out there, or who has read the 'Problems of Greater Britain,' must be aware that the Australians already show decided aspirations towards separate nationality, combined with a very ardent feeling of true patriotism (in the largest sense of the word), and with a remarkable personal attachment to the Queen and to the Prince and Princess of Wales; but they have long since passed beyond the stage of thinking themselves a part of England "as Yorkshire is a part of England." If they are not building their state on a reformed religion, in the same sense as the Puritans founded the New England colonies in the early years of the seventeenth century, they are none the less founding themselves on the evolution of a social faith in which industrialism is a vital tenet and a part of their effective religion. The lesson we have to learn is that our kin beyond the sea are giving us the lead in this direction. They are setting the step for us, not we for them; and it is this consideration which stultifies the comparison so often made, in post-prandial perorations, between the Roman and the British Empires. There is nothing more misleading than a false historical analogy.

We must never forget that, whilst there is warm affection, immense admiration, and great reverence amongst the higher elements of the New World for all that is truly admirable in the Old World, there is also exceedingly free criticism of all that is not admirable. And amongst the lower elements—amongst that large class who emigrated because they were discontented with, or rebellious against, their former lot—there is quite as much of distrust as love. If the New World has been in a certain sense the expansion of the Old World, it has also been the expansion of an "anti-Old World." The Germans in America retain still a sentiment for the Vaterland — for the land of Schiller and Goethe—but they glory far more in having got beyond "Militarismus." The English agricultural labourers or artisans in Australia, and more particularly their children, no doubt nourish a sentiment for the old home—the land of Shakespeare and Milton, the land of all the poetry, the romance, the history, the fine traditions of our race; but it is crossed with memories of a land of privilege, of inequalities of condition, low wages, slums, smoke, spirits, and a sweated residuum. It would be miserably unjust of them to fix their minds only on the latter considerations, but it is foolish optimism to believe that the former alone are held in universally loving remembrance. Their feelings are mixed, and the craving for individual expansion is as strong in a young nation as it is in a young person.

A community settled on a new continent all its own, even when the great majority of its members belongs to the same race, and even though that race be the English race, is sure almost insensibly to form new ideals, and it does not keep its gods thousands of miles away. It lives more in the hopes of its own future — of subduing the land for itself, of building its railroads, of constructing its great works of irrigation — than in the memories of ancestors in the past, however glorious. This may not be man's best estate, but it is what happens—it is what always has happened—in the history of the world.

And in thinking of the New World, we must be careful not to mix up the case of the North American and the Australasian continents with the case of Africa. Happily there is scarce the remotest possibility of the two former ever being made future battle-grounds for the Old World military powers, because England is the sole European power that now has a substantial foothold on either continent, and there is practically no aboriginal population to reckon with. On the other hand, in Africa there are six European powers—most of them conterminous one with another—all actively and jealously at work on the colonisation or exploitation of a continent already thickly peopled with an inferior and a very prolific race.

Nothing short of a miracle will prevent some of these powers from coming to loggerheads sooner or later, and then we shall see re-enacted there all the miseries — elevated, no doubt, by the heroisms — that wars have erewhile entailed upon Europe. Acquisition of territory can only be a permanent and substantial good in the cases where the acquirers can inhabit the land. Gibbon quotes a very just observation of Seneca, "Wheresoever the Roman conquers, he inhabits," and it is confirmed by history and experience. India has always been an effectual bar to the true union of a Greater Britain, and equatorial Africa will prove a second bar, because English children cannot be brought up in these countries. The only interest of the individual Englishman is to make as much money as he can out of them. He hates them and he quits them.

And it is this forward policy in a dangerous direction, this constant tendency in England to increase her already enormously extended liabilities, which is the little rift within the

lute that makes the words British Imperial
Federation anything but a fascinating strain
to great masses of voters in Canada and Australia. Evidence accumulates that they do not
dance when we pipe this tune to them. For
the truth is that they are dominated, rightly
or wrongly, by three main ideas—the sovereignty of their own people, the importance
of their own industrial development, and the
determination not to meddle with the affairs
of other people. The example of the United
States of America is very potent with them,
and in this sense it is true that American
ideas hold the field in the New World. These
ideas may ultimately prove to be not wise,
but unwise—inadequate at any rate for the
development of a higher life in a great people.
Anyhow, we may be certain that, like all ideas
of all times, they are not permanent but transitory, merely steps in the procession of ideas.
Meantime, however, they appeal to "the
masses," to the average minds, and therein
lies their present force.

America's strong points are easily seen, her
weak points are more difficult to discern and
keep in view; but her negro question, her

silver question, her very size, the unprecedentedly rapid growth of wealth (with all the peculiar temptations and degradations that quickly acquired wealth carries in its train), and the absence of a high national ideal, present their own peculiar difficulties. With her enterprising spirit and boundless resources, however, she may still be the first to arrive at a more systematic reconstruction of the social fabric than has yet been attempted; but, until she does so, her power of repelling one class of minds will be almost as great as her power of attracting another class. The cultured classes of the Old World will find more to enjoy and to admire in any corner of their own countries than in the choicest spots of the New World, but it is otherwise with those who have been the hewers of wood and the drawers of water. To them the New World is in many respects the ideal world; and in these days, when the voice of the majority is so widely recognised as the voice of God, we need not be surprised—although it may be a rude awakening—to find that Canada and the United States of Australasia will presently follow in the way that the United States of

America have led, because they imagine it to be the way of peace—the way that seems best to assure to themselves the undisturbed enjoyment of their industries, the precious possession of their individuality and the natural principle of their growth. And just as there cannot be true patriotism in the United States, in Canada, or in Australia without perpetual loyal recognition of the root from which they have all sprung — from which they have derived their language and their laws, their literature and their religion—so there cannot be true patriotism in England without proper consideration for the best interests of all the offspring; and in whatever way they see fit to work out their own future (by separation or otherwise), we shall be better occupied in strengthening our alliances and our fellowship with the whole 75,000,000 of them, in unifying the sentiment of all the English-speaking peoples, rather than in attempting a partial British Imperial Federation which, with its heterogeneous elements, can never really be welded into a homogeneous structure, because it does not represent any natural principle of growth. Even if a scheme could be evolved capable of being practically worked (and none has yet been formulated worthy of serious consideration), it would always remain a highly artificial contrivance, and would end probably in satisfying no one.

ON THE EXTENSION OF RAILWAYS IN AMERICA.[1]

EVERY one who has directed particular attention to the United States has no doubt already heard enough, and perhaps too much, of their everlasting "unprecedented material progress"; for it is an unpleasant characteristic of the less agreeable kind of Americans, that they are very apt to ram their prosperity down one's throat.

There is a story of a Yankee persistently adopting this mode of treatment to a dear, irascible British Tory of the old school, till the latter, exasperated beyond endurance, snarled out, "It's a thousand pities, sir, that Christopher Columbus ever discovered your d——d country."

[1] Fraser's Magazine, June 1873.

EXTENSION OF RAILWAYS IN AMERICA. 135

At the risk of having this impolite observation repeated, it may be again asserted that in some respects their progress really is very astounding. We have become gradually so used to big figures in the past five-and-thirty years, that we have to put ourselves back in recollection or imagination to the year 1840 to be properly impressed with the fact that America then had 17,000,000 people, and 2000 miles of railroad, built at a cost of £14,000,000. Now there are 40,000,000 people, and 70,000 miles of railroad, costing over £550,000,000, operated by some 400 separate companies or organisations, whose total earnings in the year 1871 were £80,000,000.[1] It is a curious and noteworthy fact, that this railroad mileage is as nearly as possible the same as the total European mileage for 300,000,000 people, so that in this respect the young republic has shot far ahead of the "effete old monarchies and empires." How George

[1] Now (1892) there are 65,000,000 people; 175,000 miles of railroad, costing £2,000,000,000, whose total earnings for the year 1890 were £260,000,000, operated by 1800 corporations. It may be noted that the United States have already expended exactly the amount that all the world had expended on railroads twenty years ago.

Stephenson would turn in his coffin if it could be revealed to him that the world has already spent nearly two thousand millions sterling in developing his application of steam-power—a much greater sum than all the National Debts of all the world of his day!

American railroad authorities state that 8500 miles of additional new road will be built this year (1873), and one of them gives a further glimpse into the future, saying that there are 35,000 miles more in various stages of incipiency. Therefore there would seem to be a visible supply of 113,000 miles of track. Leaving, however, the flowery paths of future imaginings, we may take it as fact that in the four past years (1869-72 inclusive) 25,000 miles of new road have been completed, inclusive of main and branch lines and sidings.

Estimating the actual cost of these at $35,000 per mile, there must have been a *bonâ fide* expenditure of cash on these new undertakings of $875,000,000, or, at exchange 133, £150,000,000. There will be a further expenditure this year of £60,000,000, making a total of £210,000,000. Now this is a very large transfer from floating to fixed capital in so short a space of time. Our largest expenditure in England on railroads was in the four years 1846-49 inclusive, when the total was £143,000,000, or an average of £36,000,000 ayear; and the largest sum in any one year was in 1848-49, £43,000,000. We know that the financial negotiations for this then unprecedentedly large expenditure precipitated on us the panic of 1847. And America has not advanced to this outlay gradually, nor by unrestricted development of her resources, without other strain on her capital or credit; for in the eight years immediately preceding 1869, the United States Government alone had borrowed £510,000,000 for war expenditures, not to mention further very large borrowings by individual States and municipalities for the same purposes.

In fact, never before in the history of the world has there been borrowing on the scale on which America has borrowed during the past twelve years. It would be very interesting to have accurate figures of the amounts taken by Europe. Estimates differ widely; but perhaps of all descriptions of securities £300,000,000 or £400,000,000 would not be out of the way for Europe's present holding. It must therefore be a very important question to large numbers of persons on this side the Atlantic to ascertain the exact nature of their investment.

There can be very little doubt about the present safety of the Government bonds; and we shall, therefore, confine ourselves to a glance at the railways only.

And in this matter we must be very careful accurately to define to ourselves the true meaning of terms. Speaking broadly, our railways in England have been built by the stockholders, and then debenture stocks have been created equal to about one-third of their cost. The position of the latter, therefore, is almost absolutely secure. There is some reason to apprehend that many English investors in the first mortgage bonds of American railroads, reasoning from analogy, suppose that these bonds are in all cases a kind of equivalent to our debenture stocks. It is of course perfectly well known to those who have cared to look into the subject, that there is in America no Government control over the relations between the cost of railroads and the mortgages upon them. Some roads are mortgaged avowedly for more than their cost; others fully up to their cost; others again for only a small percentage of their cost. Therefore whereas some bonds are merely an equivalent of an ordinary stock —where the holder takes all the risk of building the road, but is limited in his profit to a high fixed rate of interest—other bonds are as desirable investments for trust funds as can well be imagined. It is very natural that the Americans should wish to keep to themselves all the future increment of profit on their railroads; and if a bondholder is aware that he is paying the total cost of the road, and is getting in exchange a very high rate of interest for his money, there does not seem to be any decided objection to a system so carried out. There are worse ten per cent risks dealt in every day on the London Stock Exchange. But then it is very necessary that such investor or speculator should have entirely trustworthy statements of the real cost of the undertakings to guide him. He may be willing to pay the full amount actually disbursed for building and equipping a road, but he will not wish in addition to pay gigantic profits in advance to the contractors or promoters : not, at any rate, without the evidence of such payments appearing plainly on the face of the accounts. He will bear in mind that peculation and knavery have incessantly laid heavy booty on capital used in construction in its transit from a floating to a permanent condition, and that this roguery has contributed largely to swell the cost of American railroads there can be no possible doubt. A curious and instructive illustration of the fact may be found in a comparison of the cost of different lines in the same States. In Mr Poor's valuable 'Railroad Manual' for 1872-73, which in the absence of any official statistics is the most useful source of information, we find such instances as the following. These have been selected at haphazard, simply to give a general idea. It scarcely requires to be pointed out that there are many considerations, such as the acquisition of valuable real estate for terminals, &c., &c., which render anything like accurate comparisons of the cost of different roads practically impossible.

EXTENSION OF RAILWAYS IN AMERICA. 141

State.	No.	Miles.	Total stated cost.	Stated cost per mile.	Total mortgage.
ILLINOIS .	1	869	$21,500,000	$24,700	$4,500,000
	2	419	17,000,000	40,600	4,500,000
	3	219	11,300,000	51,800	7,000,000
WISCONSIN	1	80	2,000,000	25,000	1,400,000
	2	65	3,500,000	53,800	1,500,000
MINNESOTA	1	122	4,500,000	36,900	Not given.
	2	283	15,000,000	53,000	16,206,500
IOWA . .	1	118	3,700,000	31,400	1,600,000
	2	99	5,000,000	50,500	800,000
KANSAS .	1	154	5,700,000	37,000	5,700,000
	2	463	24,700,000	53,300	12,700,000
MISSOURI	1	275	8,600,000	31,300	5,800,000
	2	353	24,800,000	70,300	9,200,000
VIRGINIA	1	203	5,000,000	24,600	2,600,000
	2	428	18,000,000	42,100	11,400,000
GEORGIA .	1	259	4,100,000	16,000	680,000
	2	202	7,250,000	35,900	3,750,000
OHIO . .	1	261	11,500,000	44,000	3,800,000
	2	570	Not stated.	103,500	59,100,000

In the last-mentioned instance I have substituted the mortgage per mile for the cost per mile, and we may be sure the latter did not *exceed* the former. The above are a few examples that may be multiplied in pretty nearly every State in the Union; but for our present purposes it is sufficient to draw attention to the fact that the cost of one line is often double the cost of another line in the same State, and to the still more pregnant fact that we can find a railroad built and equipped in Georgia by stockholders at a cost of $12,500 per mile, and another road in the Far West built and equipped by bondholders at a stated cost of $136,700 a mile, with a funded debt of over $90,000 a mile.

We can further find 13 companies (inclusive of the above-mentioned) with an aggregate of 4824 miles railroad stated to cost $348,000,000, on which the total mortgages or funded debts amount to $300,000,000: an average stated cost of $72,100 a mile, and an average funded debt of $62,200 a mile. The interesting question arises, Did these roads in the aggregate cost $72,000 per mile or $62,000, or was it not a very much less sum than either? No doubt the sums stated were actually paid to some one — perhaps to a Crédit Mobilier, acting as intermediary between the directors of the railroad company and the contractors, and composed of the same shareholders—but how much went to pay for actual construction of road and equipment at first hand? The nearest approximation to an answer to this question is the assertion in America that the average expenditure on Western railways ought not to exceed $35,000 per mile for building and equipping, including those with very difficult gradients. We have seen above a first-class line of 869 miles built and equipped for $24,700 per mile. We can find others in Georgia at $16,000, and plenty more in various States at $20,000 and $25,000, and again we see them running up to $70,000 and $100,000 per mile. In some of these latter a lively business must evidently have been done by the contractors and promoters in discounting and pocketing future profits at the expense of the bondholder. Let us, however, take an instance of a road apparently built entirely with the proceeds of bonds. Here we find one in the South-west, 326 miles, with no return of cost, bonded for $6,520,000, or $20,000 per mile. Total stock, $820,000! In its first five years of existence, in what must be termed a still uninhabited region, the road has, with an average of 128 miles open, earned net $602,000 annually, or $4700 per mile. The interest on the mortgage at 7 per cent is $1400 per mile. Therefore a profit of $422,000 per annum must have gone into the pockets of the holders of $820,000 stock. If the road has done this in the "green" stage of its existence, what will it not do in the "dry," when the country it traverses becomes really populated? Its bonds, principal and interest (7 per cent), payable in gold, are quoted in New York 90 currency *asked*. That is to say, at present rate of exchange, 128 for currency, a bond of $1000 can be bought for £158, paying an annual interest of £14; principal redeemable in 1891, when $1000 gold will produce £203. Here, then, is interest at the rate of 9 per cent per annum on the investment, and a gain of £45 on £158, or about $28\frac{1}{2}$ per cent on redemption, supposing the bonds to be paid at maturity. Only 50 per cent of the gross receipts has been consumed in the working expenses of this road, whereas 60 to 70 per cent is the ordinary ratio in the Northern and Western roads, averaging nearly 65 per cent all through.

The promoters of the road bid high for money, and they show their hand in the accounts. They do not profess to have subscribed any stock further than the few hundred thousand dollars above mentioned. But they show that the net earnings per mile are already far more than sufficient to pay the interest on the mortgage per mile; and any one buying such bonds thoroughly understands that he is backing the continued prosperity of the new road—a fair risk in such a country, for which he is well paid. At any rate, if he does not so understand his position, it is his own carelessness in not investigating the accounts.

This is one instance of a fair application of the new American principle of railroad-building. The figures here seem to correspond with the facts; and there are many more in the same category. As we have seen above, there are others that are simply incomprehensible as regards stated cost. Generalising on the mass of these new American undertakings, we may say with the old Latin line, "There are good ones, a considerable number of doubtful ones, and many bad ones." Apart altogether from any question of morality, it is a most fatally mistaken policy for a country like America, that must for years continue to be a great borrower from Europe on the security of new railroads, to flood us with bonds in so many cases representing more than any actual money expended on the undertakings. It lowers the tone of all her securities, and, if persisted in, will in very truth at last kill the goose that lays the golden eggs. America has been living and growing for years on her great borrowing powers; and as long as she does it with fair decency, Europe will only be too delighted to secure the outlet for superabundant capital at tempting rates of interest. But Europe can afford to hold her hand unless the securities are trustworthy : America cannot afford even a temporary lull in the European demand for bonds : such demand ceasing, a most unpleasant commercial and financial picture presents itself to the mind's eye—" Over Niagara—and after ? " Already to the accustomed eye the craft seems working dangerously near the rapids.[1]

[1] In September of this year (1873)—six months after this article was written—the craft went over Niagara, and the "*after*" proved to be the five most lugubrious years in the commercial and financial history of the United States.

Ultimately even the heaviest bonded road, running as a trunk-line east and west, may be expected to pay its interest, the growth is so marvellous; but a very disagreeable hiatus may be conceived in the meantime.

Turning from these new roads to the older and better established, we find a mass of bonds as safe for investment as any securities in the world. We take, as instances, from Mr Poor's book, 27 roads, with an aggregate of 14,660 miles, whose total cost is stated at $613,000,000 (an average of $41,800 per mile), and whose total funded debt is $215,000,000 (an average of $14,800 per mile).

Besides these, there are millions of dollars of bonds whose relation to the cost of the roads, though not quite so favourable as the above, practically makes them very safe for investment. In fact, it is quite an exception with roads built even ten years ago to find the exaggerated mortgages of recently built roads, and in most cases it would now be impossible to duplicate the former roads at the old stated cost.

The conclusion of the whole matter as regards an investor is, that no general assertion can with truth be made about these mortgage bonds *en masse*. Each of the securities must be taken and carefully examined on its own merits, and it may always be borne in mind that the financial house negotiating their sale is apt to take a very sanguine view of possibilities. The point to most of us in investing is not the certainty of great returns twenty-five or fifty years hence, but that we may count on a punctual payment of our interest year by year.

That said, there are many opportunities, by careful exercise of judgment, to make good investments or speculations in these American mortgages, old and new, and often without extreme risk. But it will probably be found more profitable for each individual to make such ventures on his own personal examination of facts and figures than to confide the selection to a "trust company," unless he is very sure that the promoters of such trust companies have no heavy load of unmarketable securities of their own to dispose of to their shareholders. It is a fallacy to suppose that over 7 per cent can be obtained from American securities that can be compared in any fair way with English debenture stocks.[1]

It might almost have been expected that, looking to the magnitude of the interests involved, a council of American bondholders would have been organised here to obtain trustworthy reports on the various lines from independent engineers, sent out for the purpose, aided by independent local information; but a curious characteristic of the ordinary British investor is that, as a rule, he will take very little trouble to acquaint himself with the true condition of his purchases. One man buys because another man whom he knows has bought before him, and very few of them like any security except at a high price, independent altogether of its intrinsic merits.

The Germans, with their keen educated eyes, get a good deal ahead of us in monetary transactions. How heavily they laid in Five-twenty Bonds in New York, all the way from the thirties (London price) to the seventies! After that they resold them to John Bull.

[1] Alas! those halcyon days are past, never to return in the United States. It is impossible now to obtain more than $3\frac{1}{2}$ to $4\frac{1}{2}$ per cent on the best railway mortgages. What a change of credit in twenty years!

They are now attempting the same thing with the new railroad bonds.

There has been a good deal of speculation for the fall in the premium on gold entered into through these purchases of currency bonds. That is to say, one of the great inducements held out to investors has been that, looking to the spread of a quickly increasing population over an ever wider area of country, the inconvertible paper that is now redundant as a circulating medium in America will in time prove adequate only, and that its value will then approximate very closely to the value of gold.

This view would certainly appear likely to be fulfilled bar further issues of greenbacks by the Government. These issues are at present confined by law to $400,000,000, with authority to issue "such additional sum, not exceeding $50,000,000, as may be temporarily required for the redemption of temporary loans." The actual legal tender paper circulation has been as high as $433,000,000. It is now $358,000,000, but there have been very great efforts lately made to have that amount increased, and the tone of feeling in America on this subject must be very jealously watched by those who are speculating for a future approximation in value between greenbacks and gold. It is scarcely necessary to remark that the policy of expansion is abhorrent to all political economists, and to all the thinking classes in America; but expansion is a pleasant prospect to all debtors. And debtors are a very powerful class in America, where almost every man in business has a desire to possess with borrowed money more than he can own. On the other hand, the masses, whose wages do not advance in proportion to the augmentation in the price of commodities, consequent on increased circulation, and whose savings are mostly in bank in greenbacks, naturally are opposed to those greenbacks being depreciated in value—and the masses in America finally rule all policies. Meantime the state of feeling and parties is sufficiently uncertain to keep the premium at a figure that is tempting to speculators.

These are some of the aspects of the extension of American railways that may be interesting to the comparatively narrow class of investors in these securities. But there is a further view of the question. That 9000 miles of new railroad have been completed in eight new States and territories, with a population of only 2,800,000 people (or a mile of rail to every 300 people), may be but a sorry present experience for over-sanguine capitalists, but may at the same time have a much wider meaning, and a wholly beneficent effect over very much larger classes in Europe. What matters it to the labourer on Wiltshire Downs, in Essex Marshes, or in Lincoln Fens, whether mortgages bear a proper relation to cost or not? What he sees, or what he may see if any one will point it out to him, is the fact that some one has done the thing for him. And the lines laid down on the other side of the Atlantic concern him much. For what do railroads mean in a country like America, teeming with every description of mineral, agricultural, and pastoral product, where the surface wealth has scarcely yet begun to be scratched? They mean in language seemingly hyperbolical, but in fact not here exaggerated, "the potentiality of growing rich beyond the dreams of avarice." Look how the wealth has already grown. In 1790 (within the memory of still living men) the population of the States was 4,000,000, and the value of their real and personal property was estimated at £150,000,000; in 1870 the Superintendent of the Census returns population at 38,000,000, and the true value of their real and personal property at £6,000,000,000![1] And this means not only so many added dollars, but the addition of what dollars will buy, and what is too hard for the many to get without dollars—a universal education: a general consumption of literature undreamed of in the Old World; the feeling amongst all those whose mere manual labour is their only capital, that they too are equal with all other men—are a necessity to other men; that they can bargain with their employers as man to man; that they are not for ever to remain ignorant, treated to eleemosynary doles of coal or flannel in lieu of fair bargained wages; that the hope dear to men—that of ultimate independence—is no longer forbidden to them. To be sure, it may be objected that this is only one side of the picture, and a highly coloured one.

[1] Population now (1892) about 65,000,000, and the value of real and personal property about £11,000,000,000.

It will be said that the venture of emigration is uncertain; that we are insufficiently informed of the conditions of the labourer in these new countries. But do we require much detailed knowledge to arrive at a conclusion that a country possessing every variety of climate, with any quantity of land, much of it still virgin soil—3,000,000 square miles for 40,000,000 people—only requires railroads to assure conditions for manual labour impossible of attainment in any old country? As in all great movements, cases of individual suffering in emigration are unavoidable. An English labourer in Minnesota, sick unto death in a sparse-peopled region, will no doubt look back with a sigh to what he has left behind him. Here is no village green to gladden his dying eyes, nor Lady Bountiful to wipe the clammy brow with delicate handkerchief, nor parish rates to bury him. Death and sickness will be harder to him, though it is astonishing how tender he will often find his rough fellow-workers in the wilderness. But then death and sickness are not the prevailing conditions of life. The argument is the old one of stage-coaches *versus* railroads, hand-looms *versus* machinery. It is a sentimental minority argument. Lusty young fellows with lusty young wives, who are to be found by thousands among our labouring population, are not likely to be deterred from bettering themselves by fear of sickness or death, any more than they would think twice of going to India if they had enlisted in the army.

A harder life, with a prospect of ultimately rising to something higher and more independent, even accompanied by the risk of unattended sickness, is surely a preferable prospect to remaining for ever on that dreary old feudal footing of the "benefiter" and the "benefited." Surely the great general rule may be applied to almost all things under the sun—that supply will be most favourably dealt with where demand is greatest. It is a mistake, if it can be helped, to form part of a community in over-supply. Much better be part of one in over-demand.

And if on the one hand we have conjured up for a possible emigrant a dreary scene from Minnesota, may we not on the other hand dwell on the attractions of California, that Land of Promise to agricultural labourers?

Who that has seen them can forget the white painted wooden cottages, trellised with roses which grow nowhere else as they grow there? —the children as plump and rosy as the rosiest in our English lanes; the profusion of the finest vegetables, fruit, and flowers; the climate always equable by the sea; no ice nor snow—

"Soft blows the wind that breathes from that blue sky."

Miles of the very finest wheat in the world, waving beneath the forest-trees, with never a hedgerow interrupting the view, "in silence ripen, fall, and cease"; for notwithstanding that Nature has beneficently separated the wet season from the dry, so that the farmer can count on weeks when he can leave the grain ungarnered where it falls, the dearth of labour is so great that, in spite of all the marvellous mechanical contrivances of ingenious labour-saving Yankees, in every abundant year part of the crop has actually to be ploughed into the earth again. There beggary, except the beggary of decayed gentility, is unknown; there every man and woman able and willing to do hard work with their hands can not only earn good wages and comfortable living, but can finally dictate really their own terms to their employers, or, better still occupy their own homesteads.

No doubt the end attained may be mere material wellbeing. But then that is a great point to people who don't seem even likely to attain to that in England.

Watching our poor agricultural labourers here preparing for a strike, is as painful as watching a bird striking itself against the iron bars of its cage, when all the time a door is open; but the exit not being the accustomed one, and requiring some knowledge to discover it, the poor blind, helpless thing, with only a passionate consciousness of inherent right to the free air, insists on testing which is the hardest—the iron bars or its own weak body. There can be but one end to that. Here the conditions are too hopeless. Let the Union spend its money in deporting the superabundant labour, and so give the smaller number remaining behind a better chance. Let Warwickshire ponder the fact that from the year 1848, when San Francisco first really existed, till 1872, the exports from that port alone have been £250,000,000 sterling value. Let the colliers in South Wales, before they again draw on themselves the self-inflicted misery of a strike, consider that America produced in 1871, 760,000 tons of rails—just double the quantity produced in 1866, and four times the production of 1862. Last year the production was further increased, and will be again very much increased this year.[1] California is not now more than three weeks' travel from Leamington; Pennsylvania is not more than twelve days' from Cardiff. Why should English labour cut its own throat?

In this country a peculiar delight is taken by one section of politicians in pointing the finger of scorn at the political corruption in America: by another section, such corruption is sorrowfully admitted as a grievous

[1] Of all the astonishing increases in American production during the last twenty years, iron and steel beat the record. Whereas in 1870 Great Britain produced nearly four times as great a quantity of pig-iron as the United States, in 1890 the United States produced one-sixth more than Great Britain. And in Bessemer steel, Great Britain made five times as much as the United States in 1870, whereas in 1890 the United States made twice as much as Great Britain (4131 thousand tons against 2016 thousand tons). About 70 per cent of the whole production of Bessemer steel is now worked up into railway material in the United States.

blot on the institutions of a nation from which there is otherwise so much to hope for and to believe in for the future.

In this short paper we have already dwelt on the knavery practised in some of their railroad enterprises; and it may be asked, is it worth while, for a gain in material conditions, for English labourers to become citizens of a country where such things can be? Is it not better for them to remain in this land of grand old traditions, and grand old families that carry out these old traditions? The wages, to be sure, are small—15s. a-week, and meat very occasionally; but if the living is low, the thinking must be high in such an atmosphere, —where to approach a judge for the purpose of influencing his judgment, or to offer a cheque to a member of Parliament for his vote, would of itself be almost sufficient evidence to send a man to a lunatic asylum. Doubtless this is the great boast we can make in England. It is a blessing we cannot be too thankful for, nor too proud of. And it must be a profound discouragement to all lovers of republican institutions that America should have shown not one but many instances of lapsing from these inestimable virtues. But this discouragement should not be unalloyed with hope of improvement. The Irish, and latterly the negro, votes are answerable for a great deal. Education may be expected to improve them. The country is still very young, and perhaps the political corruption is not much greater than it was in England in Walpole's time. And however much we may deplore the failings of our neighbours, we are scarcely in the position to throw stones recklessly at them. For there is a kind of justice beyond the jurisdiction of Westminster Hall or Lincoln's Inn. Our Legislature has taken the people's taxes for all these hundreds of years, and yet has left millions of the population of these isles to-day absolutely uneducated, and in an ignorance so brutal that it could not be credited in America;—is that justice? The very tone adopted by a large proportion of our upper and upper-middle class people in speaking of strikes is often revoltingly unjust. It is scarcely justice that a cottager who sees a hare in his garden destroying his produce, and knocks it on the head, should be branded as a criminal, and thereby be very probably ruined for life. Nor is it exactly a thing to be proud of that in Scotland deer-forests of 100,000 acres in extent should be kept without sheep, lest sport should be spoiled; or that in England labour should be drawn from the fields to beat Norfolk stubbles or Yorkshire heather, that one noble sportsman may slaughter with his own hands some 900 birds in one day. Is the tenure of our land, or the state of our great universities, or our method of representation, free from the grossest injustice? And yet, where we have so many crying needs of reform, we are told that the burning questions of the day and the rallying-cries of a great party are the Central Asian difficulty, the maintenance of the aristocratic element in our institutions, the sacredness of endowments; and some people regard our Conservative statesmen as honestly devoting themselves to what they believe to be the best interests of their countrymen in proposing to attract the public attention mainly to such issues. But if by means of a co-operative emigration organisation our labouring classes could have conveyed to them an accurate conception of the conditions of life in America, they might perhaps be not unwilling to prove on their own vile bodies which is in reality the more corrupt state, so far as *they* are concerned.

It may perhaps be too late for those of our hewers of wood and drawers of water who are already in their prime of life to understand, even in the dimmest fashion, what the very highest privileges of being an Englishman really are; but their children in America may have a fair start with all other classes of men: they will, at any rate, all learn to read and write the language which makes all the English-speaking races kin, and which enables them all to partake equally in the noblest common traditions.

That this should be a real possibility for every class; that a nearer equality between capital and labour should be a dominant condition; that there should be the wide elbow-room that alone can annihilate caste, and that alone can give scope to the experiments that are being now tried on a small scale in England to elevate by co-operation the status of our agricultural population: these are the greater, the wider "potentialities" that every mile of new American railroad built brings a step nearer to practical attainment.

THE FUTURE OF THE AGRICULTURAL LABOURERS' EMIGRATION.[1]

At last there appears to be something very like a rainbow in the sky—a veritable arch, to join the Old World to the New—which may without exaggeration, we hope, be heralded as a perpetual promise to our agricultural labourers. It is difficult as yet to take the measure of the influence likely to be exerted on the future of emigration by Mr Arch's trip across the Atlantic; but it is almost certain to be a very great influence, probably much greater than is generally understood or acknowledged by employers in England, who seem often disinclined to look in the face the existing conditions of the white labour problem amongst the English-speaking

[1] Fraser's Magazine, January 1874.

races. Yet some of these conditions are surely very apparent and important. On the one hand, the vast continents of America and Australia, with undeveloped wealth beyond precedent, are stretching out their hands and crying aloud for the manual labourers necessary for their development; on the other hand, England is overweighted with some hundreds of thousands of these very labourers, able and willing and anxious to work, but owing to the superabundance of their numbers unable to earn wages sufficient to obtain the necessaries of life at home; with no prospect of an independent old age for themselves, nor hope that their children may attain to that deserved equality with all other classes to which they may consider themselves naturally and justly entitled, so soon as their education justifies them in claiming it.

Given the removal of certain existing hindrances, and the movement of these bodies appears to be almost as calculable as the rush of air admitted into an exhausted receiver. Such hindrances have heretofore mainly been (1) want of knowledge as to the true condition of life in the new countries;

(2) want of co-operation, and consequent dread of uprooting from the old homes, and of the isolation to be encountered in strange lands and among strange people; (3) want of money. And they have all been reasonable hindrances. The wonder really is not that so many hardy men and women have for so long neglected the opportunity of bettering themselves by emigration, but rather that so very many of them have been found to give up their village, their kinsfolk, and their acquaintance (the only experience they have ever known), to dare the terrible risks of crossing the wide seas, to often absolutely unascertained prospects of occupation and living. Immense has been the pressure of preventible suffering from the want of system hitherto prevailing in the emigration movement. But it is no doubt better that such suffering should have been experienced, and that the cure we now anticipate should have been evolved from within the labouring body itself, rather than that the attempt at systematic organisation should have been undertaken by a class or a fragment of a class outside. It is now much more likely to be

permanently successful. For the tone of the bulk of these labourers has to be raised. The belief that it is part of the immutable scheme of a Divine Providence that the hewing of wood and drawing of water is to appertain to their class as an everlasting heritage, has been transmitted to them in their blood, and they are still unmoved by the enormity of the injustice done to them by the State to whom they paid taxes, in not having earlier provided them with the opportunities of learning to read and inform themselves of the very different conditions for labour already existing elsewhere. Any little information they may have picked up about other countries has dribbled through by such circuitous processes that it has finally reached them in the most contradictory and questionable shape, so that they have not really known what to believe and what to disbelieve. And their advisers have been almost as ignorant as themselves. The average English country squires and parsons are not minutely acquainted with the details most necessary to be acquired by the intending emigrant, nor have they generally a personal knowledge of the actualities of life in new countries, so that they can scarcely be blamed for shirking the immense responsibility of taking the burden of so important a recommendation on themselves. That responsibility is so great and can so easily be appreciated, that it is unnecessary to inquire whether there has been any *arrière pensée* on the part of the squires : any interested motive of a desire not to diminish the supply of cheap labour. The fact is sufficient that there has been no wide opportunity in England for ascertaining the drawbacks and advantages offered by the various countries now competing for labour. True, there is a mass of information in regard to our colonies available in the Reports of the Commissioners of Emigration and their Colonisation Circular; but mere statistical knowledge, however well put together, will never command many readers of any class, and is of course utterly beyond the reach of the classes who cannot read. This has been the old order which is changing, and which will very shortly give place to the new. In ten words, the practical effect of Mr Arch's trip would seem to be, *the making of the labour-markets of America and England one.* It is a revolution.

The Union here, with active corresponding agencies in the principal centres of employment in the United States and Canada, will be able to disseminate through every village in England accurate information as to the demand and supply of labour and the rate of wages in every part of America. Emissaries will be sent all over the country to inform the labourers, by word of mouth and from a source they will absolutely trust, how they are to set about the removal of themselves and their belongings. Whole villages will move together, instead of single individuals; but they will not move at all until they are sent for to a fixed employment under favourable conditions. With such precautions, the former risks and suffering will be very materially diminished. If there be an exodus of these poor, illiterate people, it will be methodical, and that is a new experience in our history. Many persons in the upper and middle classes doubt whether the means will be forthcoming; but it seems to be evident that the famine of labour on the other side of the Atlantic will result in the Government of Canada, and probably in the great railroad corporations in

AGRICULTURAL LABOURERS' EMIGRATION. 169

the United States, reducing emigration expenses to a minimum, if they can make contracts for service for any reasonable length of time, as our Australian colonies have already done.[1] Independent, however, of any outside help, the force of internal organisation in such a case is almost immeasurable. We have not yet seen it fully exerted, but we may judge in part what may be done from the Irish movement after the potato famine. In the ten years 1847 to 1856, 2,800,000 persons left Great Britain without having any Mr Arch

[1] Already in June 1872, an Act was passed by the Canadian Government, dividing the Dominion into emigration districts, providing for the formation in such districts of societies for the purpose of introducing immigrants, finding employment for such as may arrive, and assisting employers to obtain the labour they require. The societies may enter into contracts, and borrow and lend money for immigration purposes, and correspond with the agents of the Dominion in the United Kingdom for the introduction of such immigrants as may be applied for, and may also take the necessary steps for recovering any advance, whether made by the society or by the Dominion agent, or by any individual in the United Kingdom, which an emigrant may have undertaken to repay. The society may also advance money to an emigrant on condition of an engagement on his part to take service with a nominee of the society for a specified period and at specified wages, and to allow the deduction from such wages and payment to the society of a sum to be fixed in the engagement.—Thirty-third General Report of the Emigration Commissioners, 1873, pp. 46 and 47.

to act as pioneer, and without any properly concerted organisation : simply driven by the pressure of hunger overmastering all obstructions. And one of the most interesting and instructive results of that movement is given in the Report of the Emigration Commissioners, stating that from 1848 to 1872 inclusive the amounts of money traced as remitted by settlers in North America to their friends in the United Kingdom amounted to £18,000,000. No doubt that is a mere indication of how those who left this country bettered themselves; it can in no sense be regarded as a measure of it. To persons who have never been in America or Australia it is very difficult to convey an accurate conception of the difference in the status of the labourer in these new countries. One would wish not " to extenuate aught or set down aught in malice." It is a misfortune that our labourers should be impressed with too rosy a view of the lands that are really in many respects lands of promise for them. There can be no question about it, that the life of the pioneer is not a comfortable life. None is much more difficult. He works harder than any English labourer has ever dreamed of doing—he suffers more from exposure—he has probably even fewer amusements—he is very solitary; but then the goal before him renders all toil endurable, and without that goal toil is scarcely a fair burden for man. He subdues the land *for himself.* He sees about him the men of his own class who have preceded him in the hard struggle, now owning their hundreds and thousands of acres; prosperous farmers with children growing up around them, reading their newspapers and their books, surrounding themselves with luxuries tending to culture (for in the house of many a well-to-do labourer who has raised himself to be a proprietor, a piano will constantly be found); his sons eligible for the Governorship of his State or for the Presidency of his country. He feels from the outset that his labour is as necessary to his employer as his employer's superior means are necessary to enable him to earn wages and experience sufficient to start for himself. The enervating system of pauperising benevolence, with the workhouse for the bourn (only preferable to the want of it, ending perhaps in actual starvation in England), is past; the more bracing, although perhaps for a time not less disagreeable process of active struggle for self, unaided by rates, but with the great hope daily growing greater of independence, has begun. And it is difficult to believe that a hard-working, enduring race of men, like the bulk of our agricultural labourers, who only require education to enable them to aspire creditably to all the dignity and independence, to all the usefulness and happiness in public or in private capacity of which human life is capable, will be content to remain deprived of these possibilities after they have thoroughly realised the knowledge that all these things are open to them or to their children within ten or twelve days' travel.

Therefore, as we are not likely to impose an export duty on our labourers, we must be prepared for a large, perhaps in a few years' time a stupendous, movement. For if it once lays hold of the imagination of our agriculturists, it will proceed in a geometrical ratio. And the majority of those who are capable of viewing the question solely from the labourer's own point of view, will not regret it, though it must needs be that the shoe will pinch somewhere in England—at any rate for a time. We confess to a great hope that it will only be a temporary pinch, for we have great faith in British capital, British science, British mechanical ingenuity, British indomitable energy, getting more out of the land than ever, spite of fewer labourers, by more scientific appliances to farming under reformed conditions of land tenure; so that the good obtained from emigration may eventually be an "all round" good. In the few words we have to say on the subject, however, our desire is rather to mitigate than to encourage enthusiastic action being taken all at once. If it is overdone before the machinery is in thorough and smooth working order, there is certain to be disappointment; for we must not forget that the great saving of immediate suffering likely to be effected by the new organisation is not without an element of danger.

In former days, only those as a rule emigrated who by a process of natural selection were the strongest and hardiest and most self-reliant. Now, many not possessed of these qualities will go, throwing the responsibility on the Unions, and they may prove themselves altogether unfit to encounter the altered conditions of life in Canada or America. Such weak brethren should take to heart before making up their minds to start, that the abstraction of any considerable number of the stronger ones will improve the wages and general status of those who remain behind. Naturally they too will move gradually and later on, unless they see a marvellous change in their condition here. And it is difficult not to be sceptical of a wide general change, until it is absolutely forced and wrung from the bulk of the property classes in this country by dearth of labour. We are aware that many persons who have the interest of the labourer most honestly and strongly at heart think and insist that he will eventually be better off here than anywhere else, and are averse to the emigration movement on patriotic grounds. Such persons argue that in England " Freedom broadens slowly down from precedent to precedent," and that it will surely reach the agricultural labourer at last. They place their hopes in a radical alteration of our system of land tenure and conveyance,—in the granting of leases to tenants—in the abolition of the laws of entail, of primogeniture, and of the game laws — in the building of better cottages by philanthropic landlords—in the system of rewarding the frugal and industrious labourer with a plot of garden for himself, or a patch of grass for his cow—or in putting ten shillings to his credit in a savings bank, in order to induce him to begin a system of laying up some provision for the future. They rightly look on it that moral reform is the first necessity, both on the part of the employer and on the part of the labourer, to the end that, in the years to come, the former will be impressed with the conviction that the profit he may earn through the sweat of the brows of other men can never rightfully belong to himself alone, but must be shared with all the producers, either in the shape of proportional wages, or in their direct participation as co-operators in the beneficial results of the work; and the latter will take the position of refusing to work except at wages sufficient to provide him with something more than mere sustenance. It may be that the thought of the civilised world is tending in this direction. We hope it is, and the highest honour is due to those who are working towards its fulfilment; but looking at the question from the standpoint of the labourer of to-day, we feel that even were the theory to be generally accepted, its practical realisation and application must be so gradual and long deferred in England, that it can scarcely be expected to have very much appreciable effect on the mass of men now concerned, whose lives are passing away day by day, whether in dull hopelessness or in newly awakened promise. Is not their most natural and proper guide an enlightened self-interest? Enlightened, we mean, in the very broadest sense, to the extent of conceiving and believing, in the noble words of the author of 'Romola,' differently applied, that "a result towards which all human goodness and nobleness must spontaneously tend is that the light abandonment of ties, whether inherited or voluntary, because they have ceased to be pleasant, is the uprooting of social and personal virtue;" and that "all minds, except such as are delivered from doubt by dulness of sensibility, must be subject to a recurring conflict when the many-twisted conditions of life have forbidden the fulfilment of a bond. For in strictness there is no replacing of relations: the presence of the new does not nullify the failure and breach of the old. Life has lost its perfection; it has been maimed; and until the wounds are quite scarred, conscience continually casts backward doubting glances."

Between employers and employed amongst our agricultural population there may be— doubtless there are — many such ties and bonds, and in these cases we surely shall not talk of "substantial good" only, as if "faithfulness and love and sweet grateful memories were no good." But a tie or a bond is loosened when either of the contracting parties has ceased to fulfil its conditions; and our argument is rather directed to those labourers who are simply regarded by their employers as instruments to be used for furnishing ways and means for game-preserving or horse-racing.

It may also be further questioned, even granting that all the reforms we have mentioned could be accomplished to-morrow, whether it would not still remain true that the excessively limited area of England must for centuries to come prevent it from offering the same inducements to the manual labourer as the practically illimitable fields of America and Australia?

As a matter of fact, too, reform moves so slowly in an old country, that an ordinary lifetime is consumed before anything is accomplished. The Hodge in prime of life in 1832, faithful to his country and his parish, who heard and understood in dim fashion from radical squire or mildly anti-conservative parson of those days, that the millennium was drawing towards him with the passing of the "Great Reform Bill," and waited expectantly for it, doubtless thinks, now that he is sixty, with children grown up as uneducated as himself, that his confidence was misplaced. He envies his neighbour, who, with perhaps unpatriotic scepticism, disbelieving in the possibility of that immediate change, imperatively demanded, in those paternal and feudal relations between employer and employed, and having a distinct determination that his future work should be for the benefit of himself, the labourer, as well as for his employer the capitalist, emigrated, and is now a prosperous farmer in America or Australia.

The Hodge of to-day, counselled by Mr Arch, is not likely to be as credulous as was his father. As a country has sown, so must it reap. Each man must judge of the crop of trust and gratitude that may be fairly expected. To us, the comfortable classes, England is "the land of such dear souls, the dear dear land;" but when asked by the sceptical for proof of the labourer being really better off elsewhere, it may confidently be asserted that it would simply be considered inconceivably retrograde for any child born in America or Australia of British labouring parents to return to the old life in the old home in the old country. Of that, we think, there can be no question, and it seems to cover all the ground of doubt. Of course there are some advantages clearly discernible in England even to the labourer. And no one can appreciate them better than one recently returned from the monotonous dreariness of Australia, or the rough unpicturesqueness of Canada and Western America, with their rude wooden shanties, dusty uninviting roads, and hedgeless fields. After them how trim our village greens look, each with its square, surrounded by white posts and chains for rustic cricketers; how inviting the clean village "public," with its sanded floor and gossip of the neighbours; how lovely the manor-houses, with their parks and lawns, "the haunts of ancient peace"; how picturesque the cottage gables covered with roses and creepers; how like a beautiful well-ordered garden the whole island is! How hard to leave it all, to be driven out from such a paradise! But it too often happens that the very conditions of the picturesque are incompatible with the most profitable husbandry: and when we examine the inner life of these cottages, how can we help wishing that the inmates could travel with the setting sun across the wide ocean till its beams slanted on the little toddlers returning home, no doubt to the roughest of shanties, but to plentiful living, from the national free schools in every village and township from Maine to California, from Quebec to British Columbia; or on the young men and maidens stacking the rich grain or driving home the kine; or on the elder folk counting their gains in land or stock, all belonging to themselves—keenly alive to the domestic politics of their adopted country; all with interests growing as the country grows; all daily bettering their conditions, with nothing before them unattainable! It is probably true, as has been remarked, that the institutions of these new countries are in advance of the intelligence of their peoples, who have not attained to them by a gradual process of evolution, but have received them ready-made from a select body of leaders. These leaders derived their experience from a knowledge of all existing polities, and in selecting that which they judged highest, were perhaps ahead of their time; and this may be one reason why we are already confronted with a condition of unprecedented political corruption, where in the beginning there was unprecedented purity. It requires perhaps a robust faith to believe that this tendency may be checked; but even in its existing evil phase it is open to doubt whether it is not better that forty million people should believe and act on the great doctrine of the equality of men, even if they should throw up a scum of four million corrupt politicians, rather than that a whole country should believe and act on the supremacy of caste. Mr Fitzjames Stephen notwithstanding, we think there is a good deal to be said in favour of equality, in this "the nineteenth century since the Man Divine taught and was hated in Capernaum." Hated!—why? Chiefly on account of His preaching that doctrine. At any rate, so far as our agricultural labourers are concerned, they will surely gain more than they will lose by it, even if all the drawbacks asserted to proceed from the system are admitted.

And it must not be forgotten that in his visit to Canada, Mr Arch has only yet accomplished one-half of his task, and that, in our opinion, the less important half. Putting aside for the moment all question of nationality, it can scarcely be maintained that a country with so long and rigorous a winter is as eligible for emigrants as many of the Western States of America. No doubt Canadians will stoutly affirm that it is preferable. But we gain a piece of information from the United States census of 1870, which appears to dispose shortly of the arguments on the subject, and carries more weight than all mere assertions that can be made. Out of the total foreign-born population of 5,600,000 in the United States, more than one-twelfth, or exactly 495,000, were born in British North America; and as the population of Canada was 3,700,000 at the census of 1871, it would seem as if about one-eighth of the Canadians preferred the States as a residence. Great as is the prosperity of Canada, we think that any unprejudiced Englishman in crossing the border must acknowledge that the prosperity of the United States is greater; and taking into consideration the very much milder climates to be found there in more southern latitudes than Canada, we cannot help believing that they afford an altogether preferable field for emigration. It is evident that the bulk of emigrants find it so. Taking the figures of the total emigration from Great Britain for the last ten years, from 1863 to 1872 inclusive, we see that the total number of persons embarked was 2,300,000, of whom 1,749,000 (or 76 per cent) were destined to the United States; 232,000 (or 10 per cent) to North American colonies; 242,000 (or 11 per cent) to Australia; 79,000 (or 3 per cent) to elsewhere. Or again, if further proof be wanted, we find that "the total number of emigrants who arrived in the United States during the fiscal year ended June 30, 1873, was 459,803 (404,806 the previous year), of whom 307,334 landed at New York, and 58,917, WHO CAME THROUGH CANADA, entered the country at Huron, Michigan."

The considerations by which emigrants are naturally influenced in giving a preference to one destination over another, where wages are about the same, and where language is identical, are :—

1. *Climate* most suitable to their constitutions and to agricultural employment. Cheap land, and plenty of it, with the greatest facility for marketing produce.

2. *Accessibility.* — As short a period of travel, especially of sea travel, as possible.[1]

3. *Political and social considerations,* in-

[1] Of the emigrants to North America in 1872, 261,846, equal to 98.04 per cent of the whole, went in steamers, and only 41.06 in sailing-ships. The proportion of those who go in steamers has shown a continuous increase since 1863, when it amounted to less than 46 per cent of the whole. The shorter passage and

cluding nationality.—If the advantages and the drawbacks appertaining to each destination are put fairly and fully before the intending emigrant, and if he of his own freewill, and after due consideration, deliberately prefers to retain his nationality and his allegiance, rather than gain certain advantages by becoming the citizen of another country, every Englishman must rejoice at and admire the patriotism of his decision. Certainly none of us would be found to discourage him. But it is difficult to see anything either to rejoice at or to admire in those who counsel a destination other than the most desirable, without letting the totally uneducated emigrant know on what grounds the conclusion has been arrived at, very often involving him in all the

the better accommodation of the steamers make up for the additional cost.

The resort to steamers has also much diminished the mortality on the voyage. Among 230,531 emigrants on 545 voyages to North America of which we have received returns, the deaths were only 102, which, taking the voyage at twelve days, is equal to a mortality of only 13.38 per 1000 per annum. Considering the effect which the change of life and sea-sickness are calculated to have on the feebler members of the emigration, such a rate of mortality must be admitted to be very low.— Thirty-third General Report of the Emigration Commissioners, 1873, p. 3.

misery of a second emigration. It is most important to him that he should get to the most suitable place in one move, and he surely ought to be the sole judge of the extent of his own patriotic feelings; besides, it is not a necessity in all the States that he should become an American citizen simply because he is a landowner. Take an instance even in our own class. If an English gentleman in very needy circumstances were offered the choice of a tolerably good appointment in Montreal, or a more lucrative one in New York or Boston, in which latter places he might see superior advantages in openings for his children, we do not believe his friends would recommend him, on patriotic grounds, to decline the more valuable appointment; and even if his friends did (who are sometimes patriotic, like Artemus Ward, to the extent of "sending all his wife's relations to the war!"), we are pretty confident that the gentleman himself, if he had wife and family, would postpone to what he considered their best interest considerations of residence, and possibly even of nationality. We do not wish to push the argument too far; but reflect on the difference between the gentleman to whom England may be a real paradise, and the agricultural labourer to whom it certainly is not, and let us modify any accusation of want of patriotism : if that is to be charged at all, let it be put on the right shoulders—viz., on that portion of our hereditary aristocracy and "gorgeous plutocracy" who are apparently willing to sacrifice all the prosperity and good feeling of the country for their unbridled lust of sport.

Taking into account the reasons we have mentioned above as ruling the choice of destination, it appears to us that Canada is at an irremediable disadvantage as regards the first (climate); and until time and space are annihilated (or the governing markets of the world are changed), our Australian colonies will not be able to compete on equal terms under the second of these requirements (accessibility). As regards the political and social considerations, it would take a longer examination than we have space for here to weigh the inducements held out respectively by the three great competitors for our surplus labour; but it may be doubted whether there is any sufficient superiority in any one of them over any other, to alter a determination arrived at, from the remaining considerations, by an English agricultural labourer.

President Grant, in his last inaugural Message, threw out an idea of a great future Federation, which was received with a good deal of mocking derision in England. But there may be a notion more grotesquely absurd than that the people on the American continent, who all speak the same language, and are mainly governed by the same laws, should eventually have but one custom-house (let us hope for collection of duties for revenue purposes only!), one post-office, one central executive and—shall we say it?—finally one nationality. There is not probably to-day the bitterness of feeling between the Canadians and Americans that existed between Scotsmen and Englishmen before the Legislative Union a hundred and seventy years ago; and yet it is almost impossible to find now the faintest remnant of that bitterness in Scotland. Identity of interests and constant inter-communication, and the feeling that union was inevitable, have absolutely erased it. Is it not wiser to hope that this same tendency may increase on the other side of the Atlantic, rather than encourage the feeling of national hostility between peoples who ought to have no divergent interests? Meantime, we think that the British agricultural labourer proposing to emigrate ought to have the fullest and most unprejudiced information laid before him about both countries, so that he can make a reasonable election, knowing the advantages and the drawbacks. Until Mr Arch has visited and reported on the various States in the American Union, probably the most reliable knowledge may be derived from the 'Reports from her Majesty's Consuls of the manufactures, commerce, &c., of their consular districts.' What a world of information, for instance, we obtain in the following half-dozen lines in the report of Consul Booker, upon California for the year 1871: "The savings and loan societies of San Francisco had on deposit on 31st December, £7,406,675 on account of 41,590 depositors, against £6,257,910 on account of 36,862 depositors on the previous 31st December. It will be seen that the average amount to each depositor was £178, against £169 in 1870."

The population of San Francisco in 1870 was 150,000, and of the whole State of California 560,000. Of this population 91,176 attended school, and only 24,877 persons over ten years of age in the whole State could not read, and only 31,716 of all ages (including 2853 Chinese and 1789 Indians) could not write. Five-and-twenty years ago the site of the city was an agglomeration of sand-hills, with a single Spanish mission-house, and the State was only the home of a few Indians. We must find space for the following further extract from the same report:—

"Great efforts are now being made to increase our agricultural population, and it can only be for want of knowledge of the advantages California offers to the settler that keeps it so very limited. Every man with any knowledge of farming and with a small capital, can without difficulty secure a homestead for himself and family, and his future success depends upon his own exertions. The drawback to success, where there have been failures, has been the result of careless farming. The facility for growing grain is so great, that the raising of wheat and other

cereals has been in too many instances alone the object of the farmer; whilst the mere fact that during the time the grain is growing there is comparatively nothing to be done, should induce farmers to add to their grain-growing, stock-raising and garden-farming. The State Board of Education very properly calls the attention of the farmers to the benefits to be derived from keeping a few head of sheep and cattle on their farms to eat their grain straw in preference to burning it, which is the practice in many parts of the State. It points out to them that this straw, eaten and trampled by the cattle, may be a source of direct profit, in furnishing our markets with beef and mutton where they are most poorly supplied, and where they command the highest prices, and also in contributing to the producing qualities and fertility of the soil, which, however rich now, will in a few years of constant cropping and no manuring be reduced to a state of poverty and unproductiveness.
. . . The production of fruits of all descriptions, except strictly tropical, is enormous, and the drying of figs and raisins has become a business of considerable importance. Grapes,

pears, and peaches have been sent in some quantities to the Eastern States."

The average daily wages in California, without board, vary from one dollar seventy cents, or, say, seven shillings in winter, to two dollars fifteen cents, or, say, nine shillings in summer, for ordinary field hands. The present writer had personal experience of that delightful State ten years ago, but distrusts his own recollection of figures showing the astounding scale on which farms there are worked. The Philadelphia 'Public Ledger,' however, states that "one field in Livermore Valley, in California, covers 68,000 acres, or over 106 square miles, and has yielded over 40 bushels of first-class wheat to the acre." And "in the San Joaquin Valley there is a field of 100,000 acres!"

The whole of the Report of Consul Kortright on the trade and commerce of the States of Pennsylvania, Ohio, Illinois, Indiana, Iowa, Michigan, and Wisconsin, for the years 1870 and 1871, is also well worth studying for those who take an interest in emigration. We can only find space for one extract:—

"The State of Michigan is another example

of the great increment in population in the Western States, chiefly by immigration. In 1830 its population numbered less than 32,000. According to the census of 1870 it now has 1,184,296. The southern portion of the State consists of rich prairies studded with oak and watered by many rivers, favoured by a mild climate. The railroads and numerous lakes and rivers render its navigation facile. The price of improved farms averages from £2 to £20 an acre, according to situation. Unimproved lands can be bought for 4s. to £20, the higher prices ranging only when the land is cleared, fenced, or well wooded. All kinds of labour, skilled and unskilled, find a ready market, especially farm hands, wood-choppers, and common labourers. Wheat costs from 3s. 2d. to 5s. per bushel; corn, 2s. to 3s. 2d.; oats, 1s. 4d. to 3s. 5d.; potatoes, 1s. 3d. to 4s. Small farmers can do well in the counties of Ottawa and St Clair, where wild land can be purchased at from £1 to £4 per acre, with one to ten years to pay it in, at 7 per cent interest. There is still a vast field for immigrants of all kinds in this State, as land is abundant, the communications numerous, and Government lands especially can be obtained cheap. Mining also offers a vast field for industrial occupation. . . . The average rates of wages are as follows for farm-labourers:—

	Per month, with board.
Experienced hands in summer	£4 16 3
Experienced hands in winter	3 12 7
Ordinary hands in summer	3 12 9
Ordinary hands in winter	2 17 11
Common labourers at other than farm work	4 4 6
Female servants	1 17 11

"Where the labour is engaged without board, it averages in the case of farm hands about 16s. per month higher than the above rates. Farm hands are also largely engaged by the day, especially in summer."

We have preferred making the above extracts from our own consuls' reports, because we think they are more likely to be received in this country as unprejudiced than any information coming from a purely American source; but for any one desirous of acquiring the greatest amount of information in a compendious and, we believe, entirely trustworthy form, there is a most interesting little volume compiled by the Hon. Edward Young, Ph.D., Chief of the Bureau of Statistics, and published at the Government Printing Office, Washington, 1872. It is entitled, 'Special Report on Immigration; accompanying information for immigrants relative to the prices and rentals of land, the staple products, facilities of access to market, cost of farm-stock, kind of labour in demand in the Western and Southern States,' &c. &c., to which are appended tables showing the average weekly wages paid in the several States and sections for factory, mechanical, and farm labour; the cost of provisions, groceries, dry goods, and house-rent in the various manufacturing districts of the country in the year 1869-70.

Our purpose, however, is not to advocate any particular country or State, but rather to advise the labourers to pause until they have further materials from which to draw conclusions as to the desirability of all the destinations offering, and not to move at all except to fixed engagements. We cannot but look on the emigration movement as a good and healthy movement for all parties concerned. We expect to see the small farmers, without sufficient capital, finding out, too, that when wages rise it will be for their interest to seek the new lands, where they will be men among men, instead of being condescendingly admitted to a sort of *quasi*-equality with the neighbouring squire at cover-side, or among the turnips at home. These movements may lead in time to the reforms noticed at the beginning of this paper, which it may be hoped will be carried out without any violent recrimination or bandying of reproaches among classes. An enlightened self-interest on the part both of employers and employed—embracing the proposition, *non pour nous seuls, mais pour tous nous naissons*—will probably guide us safely through them. One word we must say in regard to the existing prostration of trade in America. To any one who had noticed carefully the progress of the country, it has for some time past been evident that the extension of its railroad enterprises was too rapid. The consequence has been a financial panic, very similar to that of 1847 in England. Many manufactories have been closed. There is widespread distress among the factory hands and among artisans in general this winter. Of these classes, we shall probably see a good many who have lately left this country returning. The most will be made of such a movement by the Anti-Emigration party. Let not the agricultural labourers, however, be misled. These 25,000 miles of railroad which have been built in the past four years, and are mainly accountable for the financial confusion, *must* be good friends to them.

Finally, we have great hopes that the deep-sea cables, which have up to this time been used almost exclusively by the rich classes, and have effected principally an equalisation of profits and losses in trade, may, by lighter and cheaper construction, be made available for equalising all conditions; so that the rich will not grow so rapidly and unwholesomely rich, and the poor will grow richer. We hope to see ten words sent across the Atlantic for a dollar—4s. 2d.; and those who know the horror that partially educated people have of writing a letter, and the way the uneducated will shirk the trouble of getting it written, will appreciate the difference to them of going to the nearest telegraph office and getting the operator to tinkle the bell in their native village in England, and announce, " Doing finely: bring father and mother : more the better here."

AMERICA REDIVIVA.[1]

THE return to specie payments, if safely effected on the 1st of January, will make an epoch in the history of the United States and a great moral tradition for the people. The accomplished fact will enkindle belief in all reform and progress, and will falsify the predictions of the prophets (and they were many) who foretold that the democracy would never submit to the great sacrifices necessary to raise the value of all debts from 38 cents in 1864 to 100 cents to-day. A recent instance will prove what a crucial test this has been. In June 1864, an Englishman lent £10,000, or its then equivalent, 120,000 dollars, on mortgage on an American farm worth 400,000

[1] Macmillan's Magazine, January 1879.

dollars. The loan has just been repaid, and the 120,000 dollars produces £24,500. Thus his *profit* has been £14,500, *besides* interest during the fourteen years at the rate of 6 per cent per annum to start with, increasing to 14½ per cent per annum with the rise in value of the currency. What he, as a creditor, has gained in this way, his unfortunate American debtor has lost. There can be no doubt of the hardship of such a case. Here truly is an "unearned increment of value" almost sufficient to justify the expression "bloated capitalist!" And this is the real meaning of resumption. It is of course true that depreciation is equally hard on all creditors, and if the two processes concerned the same individuals the results might be equalised and no great harm done. But as a matter of fact this never can be so; and I think it redounds to the credit of universal suffrage that each time hard or soft money has been fairly brought to a popular vote the people have been true to themselves, notwithstanding all that the most skilful and unscrupulous demagogues could urge to seduce them. The honesty evinced at the polls is the more striking when it is remembered that one person out of every four in the United States has both a foreign father and a foreign mother, and that *their* patriotism, therefore, cannot have very deep roots. Not to mention English and Scotsmen, there are almost as many Germans as Irishmen, and these are not always the best specimens of their nationalities, while a very great number of them went to the country as professed socialists. The welding of this immense foreign mass into the native metal is a very trying process, and must ever be borne in mind in criticising American proceedings. After resumption, it will be difficult even for pessimists altogether to despair of the Republic. We have known something of the difficulties of paper money in England, and so lately as 1835 Mr Mill found it necessary to adopt very severe language in denouncing the "currency juggle" here.

But the birth-throes of resumption were not the only cause of the bad times and suffering which have been experienced in America during the last five years; and it may be useful rapidly to run over the period between 1862 and 1873 before proceeding to notice the later events which have conduced to a very considerable revival of soundness and prosperity.

The root of the evil was the destruction of capital during the civil war, which may be measured, in some sense, by the withdrawal of a million and a half of soldiers from active production, and the annihilation of all industry and of a vast amount of property in the Border and Southern States. These influences were not felt in their full force at the time in the North, owing first to the issue of 400 million dollars inconvertible legal tender paper-money, and afterwards to the extraordinary amount of borrowing. The immediate effect of the large issues of paper was to make all debtors "feel good," as they say in America. The appended table will show what the 100 dollar greenback was worth in gold on 30th June of each of the years following 1862 :—

1861	100	1870	85·6
1862	96	1871	89·0
1863	76·6	1872	87·5
1864	38·7	1873	86·4
1865	70·4	1874	91·0
1866	66·0	1875	87·2
1867	71·7	1876	89·2
1868	70·1	1877	94·5
1869	73·5	1878	97·3

Any statement of figures, however, can give but a limited idea of the bad effect on all kinds of business, and the widespread demoralisation incident to the violent daily and hourly fluctuations in the value of the circulating medium. The way in which mercantile transactions were carried on in the second largest commercial city in the world, for several years after the suspension of specie payments, was certainly most curious, and, in looking back on it, it appears already like a dream. Up to 1867, if my memory serves me right, there was no Gold Clearing Bank in New York; and up to the end of 1865 there was no bank that would take gold on deposit and let cheques be drawn against it. The consequence was that all the gold bought and sold for the first four years after suspension was delivered from office to office in bags containing £1000 each. These used to go round and round from buyer to seller —shovelled in and out again, generally in a few minutes' time—just sufficient to test their weight in a very rough-and-ready way. It was a striking instance of the difficulty of a community suddenly accommodating itself to new conditions. No city in the world had better banking accommodation than New York: nowhere was the economy of labour by the use of cheques and clearing better understood or more fully acted on. But when business had to be done in two currencies instead of one, the requisite facilities could only apparently be developed by slow and gradual stages. First, the bags of gold going round, as in primitive races; then, after some years, cheques; lastly, after some more years, clearing: a beautiful example for students of evolution! Transactions on a large scale in gold did not begin till about the end of July 1862, when the price rose rather suddenly to 120. This advance made it evident that all mercantile operations must of necessity be kept on a specie basis, by immediate sales of gold against all produce shipped, and by purchases of gold against all sales of goods imported. A forced paper currency might be a local standard of value in America, but all her external trade operations had to be finally adjusted to the world's standard. This necessitated immense dealings in gold, and speculation aiding it, the premium advanced by leaps and bounds. In June 1864 the highest price of 280 was touched; that is, it took 280 paper dollars to buy 100 gold dollars. On the day that sales were made at 280 in the morning, the price fell later in one drop to 255, and at three o'clock the same afternoon it was offered at 225. From this it will be seen at a glance that any one who borrowed 100,000 dollars gold in the morning and sold it at 275, could have bought it back the same evening at 225, netting 50,000 dollars currency profit on the operation. This is a sample (no doubt an extreme one) of daily fluctuations which went on for months and years. Conducting business under these circumstances was like driving a high-pressure engine, and sitting on the boiler without a safety-valve.

When money was liable to be made or lost in such amounts in every necessary transaction, the use of working became less and less obvious. How could any really legitimate mercantile operations be entered into under such conditions of uncertainty? A cargo of tea or coffee might be sold at a most satisfactory price in currency, but before the vendor could get from his place of business in South Street to Exchange Place, where he had to buy his gold, a rise or fall in the premium would upset all calculations. So, too, with exports of produce, paid for by bills drawn on Europe. Everything depended on how the gold was sold. The uncertainty was even greater in Philadelphia, Baltimore, or St Louis; since New York alone had a gold exchange, where all the business of the country concentrated. This being so, many merchants turned their attention to trying what could be made by buying and selling gold, pure and simple, without complicating the transactions with merchandise. This was fatal in its simplicity and in the habits it formed; for the step from gambling in gold to gambling in stocks, or anything else, is a very short one. There is, too, at all times a peculiarly speculative element in the ordinary American man of business. He fears the ups and downs of life less than the ordinary European. Excitement is more pleasing to him than any small certainty. He is fond of exercising the sharpness of his wits, and in the fluctuations of the currency opportunities were boundless. The result was that gambling became a predominating national vice, with the sure concomitants of excessive extravagance in living and in general expenditure. New York ran riot. Rents were doubled and trebled. The number of private carriages increased tenfold. So morbid was the craving for perpetual excitement, that a stock and gold exchange was in active operation "uptown," at the Fifth Avenue Hotel, then the centre of what may be called the West End of the city. Nor was the fever confined to New York. It permeated every city of the Union. The only people who really seemed to feel poor were the wealthy. It looks like a paradox, but it is a fact. The man with £80,000 out on safe mortgages, who before the war got his £5000 a-year interest, and spent it, found his income gradually going down to £4000, £3000, £2000; that was the decline if, for instance, he was living in Europe, and it had to be remitted; or, what amounted to the same thing, the currency price of commodities increased to that extent in America. On the other hand, to make quite sure of growing rich, it was only necessary to borrow currency and to buy gold, stocks, merchandise, houses, land—any property, in short. And the more any one borrowed the richer he got. It was well, therefore, to do it *en gros*. Finally it came to this, that nearly every one began to think, and to end by stating, that he was "worth a million dollars!" It was so easy to make, apparently. Thus it will be understood how, even during the existence of the civil war, the whole mass of the people in the North who were debtors felt themselves better off.

The farmers got high currency prices for their products, and as they were mostly in debt to their mortgagees, they seemed to be coining money. The shopkeepers who bought goods on credit in currency found them constantly advancing in value on their hands. And the moment the war was ended, gigantic borrowing began. It is estimated that between 1865 and 1873 America got from Europe between £300,000,000 and £400,000,000 from sales of Government, State, City, and Railway bonds. This no doubt went a long way to fill up the vacuum of capital caused by the war. And in the five years ending with 1873, over 28,000 miles of new railroad were constructed at a cost of £280,000,000, so that the demand for labour was at high pressure, and a vast mass of labourers who had been engaged in the war were quietly absorbed back into productive employment. This put off the day of reckoning, because it is easy to pay high wages with borrowed money.

But the sudden pouring in of immense amounts of new capital is always a very dangerous process in any country, as we have since seen in the payment of the war indemnity to Germany by France. It is very apt to sap the morality of a people, and it will be understood that the morality of the American people had already been pretty well sapped. No nation could have been subjected to more demoralising influences than those accompanying the advance in gold from par to 280 in three years, and the decline from 280 to 130 in the five following years. It was in September 1869 that Messrs Jay Gould and Fisk concocted the great gold "ring," which was the dying kick of the expiring gold excitement, when in three days the price was forced up from 137 to 167, and back again to 132.

This was one of the most successful and disgraceful "corners" ever effected in Wall Street. It came to a head on "Black Friday," the 24th September, when these stock-gamblers, having all the available gold in their own hands, locked it up, and made it impossible for those who had sold to make deliveries under their contracts except at the conspirators' own price. Many an honest man was ruined by that single day's work; and that so many of them should have paid out their last dollar rather than fail on their contracts, shows how binding is that outside conscience, derived from a custom of trade, which will not admit that even such a conspiracy can be pleaded in bar of the fulfilment of obligations. The clearings for the three days were said to amount to one hundred millions sterling, and it took weeks to get the accounts straight. The "corner" was only broken in the afternoon by a telegram from Washington ordering the assistant treasurer to sell gold for immediate delivery. Even personages very high in the Republic were said not to be free from complicity in the whole transaction. If the rose itself was pure, those who dwelt very near indeed to the rose were unquestionably tainted. Corruption was in the air. It grew with what it fed on. Between 1868 and 1873 there were "corners" in everything: in stocks, in grain, in cotton. There was the famous "day of the three corners" in 1872, when $\frac{5}{8}$ per cent was paid for the loan of money, $\frac{3}{8}$ per cent for the loan of gold, and $2\frac{1}{2}$ per cent for the loan of Erie stock *for the one day*. Riches were supposed to be made by one man getting his profit out of another's loss. Tweed was robbing the city. Credit Mobilier scandal in connection with the Pacific Railways had come to light, and a judge in New York was issuing blank injunctions to the most notorious stock-gamblers. The money market was in a state of constant spasms. Day after day, for weeks and months together, borrowers were paying $\frac{1}{8}$ to $\frac{1}{4}$ per cent commission *per diem*, besides interest at the rate of 7 per cent per annum for loans. This could not last. The fruit had got to that stage which succeeds ripeness, and fell. The failure of Jay Cooke & Co., on 19th September 1873, followed by a string of houses who had been occupied in financing the new railroads, was the point of apparent origin of the panic; but, as I have endeavoured briefly to point out, the whole catastrophe was in reality a slowly prepared growth of the entire character of the business of the country. Following these finance houses, railways, mercantile firms, and savings banks became bankrupt in rapid succession, and to such an extent that credit may be said to have ceased to exist. During 1873 the price of gold ranged from 119 to 107. The currency price of commodities which had followed the upward movement in the gold premium had not kept pace with its decline. By the end of the year hundreds of thousands of workmen had been thrown out of employment by the breaking of that small wheel of credit which keeps all the big wheels of production and transportation turning. This of course affected the demand for every article of consumption, and the distributing merchants throughout the country felt the pinch, not only of this smaller actual demand, but also found that their stocks of goods laid in at the high currency prices were constantly shrinking in currency value owing to the appreciation of greenbacks. Shrinkage was universal. To add to the depression, the harvests of cereals in 1870-71 and 1871-72 had been below an average, and the farmers felt the growing burden of their loans.

The figures representing the external trade of the country from 1863 to 1873 are instructive. The net imports of merchandise (that is, the total imports, less imported goods afterwards exported to foreign countries) amounted to £890,000,000; the exports of domestic merchandise in same period were £665,000,000; so that in these ten years the imports of merchandise exceeded the exports (exclusive of specie) by the enormous total of £225,000,000. During the same period the exports of coin and bullion (all the gold in the country having been driven out of circulation by the paper issues) exceeded the imports by £135,000,000, thus leaving a balance of £90,000,000 imports in excess of exports of merchandise and specie combined. But, as we have seen during this very time, there was an ever-growing interest account to be remitted to Europe for the £300,000,000 or £400,000,000 raised on loans, so that American exports ought to have exceeded imports by at least £30,000,000 annually. Instead of this, there was £90,000,000 the other way in ten years. This fact led Professor Cairnes, in 1873, to the conclusion that the condition of the external trade of the United States was essentially abnormal and temporary. "If that country," said he, "is to continue to discharge her liabilities to foreigners, the relations which at present exist between exports and imports must be inverted. Her exports must once again, as previous to 1860, be made to exceed her imports, and this by an amount greater than the excess of that former period in proportion as her financial obligations to foreign countries have in the interval increased. This, it seems to me, is a result which may be predicted with the utmost confidence. The end may be reached either by an extension of exportation or by a curtailment of importation, or by combining both those processes; but by one means or other reached it will need to be. It is simply the condition of her remaining a solvent nation."

The news of the commercial crisis in New

York reached Professor Cairnes as he was writing these words, so soon to be completely and emphatically confirmed by the subsequent facts.

Up to the very eve of the crash in America this gigantic excess of imports was being triumphantly pointed to as showing the wonderful spending power of the country. It was not heeded that it was capital being expended as if it were income. The old fallacies in regard to the balance of trade are no doubt exploded; but we may be in danger of an equally misleading fallacy in believing that the fact of a country's imports exceeding its exports is to be taken as a sign of prosperity. No such general statement can in truth be made; and if made, it can only be accepted with the strictest limitations. The phenomena cannot be isolated in this way. The relation of the exports and imports must be considered in connection with the profitableness or otherwise of the general trade of the country. We have seen that in America the excess of imports was the prelude of the greatest adversity.

The years 1874 to 1877 will long be remembered as a period of unparalleled suffering amongst all the dwellers in the cities of the United States. The great trunk railroads went to war with one another, owing to the excessive competition for a limited amount of business which they had all been spending vast sums of money to control. Rates were cut down to a point at which a great deal of the through business was done at an absolute loss. Transportation was reduced to an absurdity (to the transporters), when 100 lb. of wheat was carried by the lakes and canals from Chicago to New York—fifteen hundred miles—for sixpence! Many of the railroads, too, had undertaken the business of collieries: one of them in its report some years ago mentioned the borrowing of £2,400,000 to secure sufficient coal lands to give the road employment in transportation for centuries, and after that borrowed £12,000,000 more in England to develop these lands, on the anticipation, no doubt, that America was going to construct 10,000 miles of new railroad every year to eternity. Instead of this, the construction of new railroad has scarcely been 2000 miles a-year since 1873. The consequences to the coal and iron industries may be imagined. All the dependent industries of course became affected, and there were never so many unemployed labourers at any one time in the United States. They swarmed over the country—a menace to society.

The lowest point of general depression was about coincident with the lowest price of railroad stocks—namely, in the first half of 1877; and some idea may be formed of the depreciation in this class of property between 1873 and April 1877, when it is mentioned that such stocks as Central of New Jersey had fallen from 120 to 6; Illinois Central from 116 to 40; Chicago and North Western (ordinary) from 80 to 16; Michigan Central from 110 to 34. The cause was not far to seek. The number of inhabitants to a mile of railroad was 925 in 1867, and only 577 in 1876. It was a question of the survival of the fittest lines. The weak ones had to go into liquidation. The extent to which their construction had been carried in advance of their profitable employment, may be judged from the fact that the £633,000,000 invested in United States railway property before 1872 brought in just the same net earnings as the £913,000,000 invested in 1877!

To save expenses the wages of the employees had been greatly reduced, and the bad times came to a climax with the widespread railroad strikes in Pennsylvania in August 1877. And for a short time these strikes looked most threatening to the cause of law and order throughout the States. The destruction of life and property was very considerable, but the difficulty was more easily overcome than was at one time expected. For it is true, as has been so often observed—and it must never be forgotten in attempting to judge American issues—that the mass of real American people is pre-eminently law-abiding and law-enforcing.

With decreasing profits of industry in every branch of trade, and the immensely increased taxation,[1] there was really only one course possible to recover national prosperity. That

---

[1] Governor Tilden in his message to the New York State Legislature in January 1876, mentioned that in 1870 the taxes —Federal, State, and local—of the whole country amounted to £146,000,000, against £31,000,000 in 1860; or reducing the figures to a *per capita* comparison, the taxes were £3, 16s. per head in 1870, against £1 per head in 1860.—Martin's Statesman's Year-Book.

course was national economy. And it was pursued. There is an old saying that "when America takes to wearing her old shoes she can lay the world under contribution." This is what has happened. There is probably no other nation that has the same capacity for suddenly restricting a profuse expenditure. New York, so lately riotous, became a pattern of quiet living. People talked poor and lived poor. It became a fashion. It was like the case we sometimes see of a wildly extravagant bachelor suddenly settling down to the cares of married life with a thoughtful prudence astonishing to his most intimate friends.

The value of fancy goods, silk goods, jewellery, and precious stones, imported in 1877, was £5,000,000 less than in 1873; the consumption of coffee in same period fell off $2\frac{1}{2}$ lb., and of tea 1 lb., per head of population. These are fair samples of what was going on throughout the country in diminished consumption of articles of luxury. But this forced economy told both ways for some time on the general condition of trade. It was a negative more than a positive advantage.

But there was also a positive and much

more potent cause of prosperity actively at work, though not so visibly. The crops of cereals from 1872-73 onwards, proved abundant and ever-increasing (with the exception of the Indian-corn crop, 1874-75, and a partial failure of the wheat crop in some of the North-Western States in 1876); and in 1877, concurrently with the largest production up to that time, the threatening position of political matters in the East of Europe, and the falling off of supplies of grain from Russia, gave the American farmers a great chance, of which they were not slow to avail themselves. There was heard the ceaseless tread of a vast army of emigrants from the Atlantic and middle States, and from Europe to the Far West,—and that army saved the situation.

And here we may take notice of the fact that, although the making of all these new railroads had been, generally speaking, a most unpleasant experience to the capitalists, both native and foreign, it brought an immense area of country within the reach of markets, so that there was the very great compensation of one set of people in the country gaining what another set in *and out of* the country lost. It was not like the case of England lending hundreds of millions sterling to defaulting foreign governments, where the loss was absolute, like so many sovereigns cast into the sea, never to be recovered again. America had this advantage in being a debtor country, that other nations contributed to her losses, whilst she alone reaped all the benefits of the resulting low prices. The railroads exist, and must be a gain to the country for all time. The very low rates of transportation, which looked so disastrous from the stockholders' point of view, permitted vast masses of bread-stuffs and provisions to be made available for consumption, that otherwise would have been wasted. Mr Poor, the American railroad statistician, estimates the saving in movement of 200,000,000 tons of freight, by the improved facilities made in the railroad system during the past twenty years, at £200,000,000 *per annum;* and the Director of the Bureau of Statistics has lately stated that the total traffic on four railroads—the New York Central, the Lake Shore, the Pennsylvania, and the Fort Wayne—is, in his belief, considerably greater in value than the entire foreign commerce of the United States, imports and exports combined.

Here, then, were the elements of the most certain prosperity : the largest production ever known, the lowest carrying rates ever known, and, owing to circumstances in the East of Europe, exceptionally good prices for grain and provisions. This year's production has again been greater than anything known before, and a very few figures will illustrate the marvellous growth in three of the great staples :—

Production.		1860.	Average of five years, 1870-75.	1878.
Wheat	qrs.	22,000,000	33,000,000	50,000,000
Indian corn	,,	104,000,000	120,000,000	162,000,000
Cotton	bales	4,800,000	3,300,000	5,200,000

And, as a consequence of this increase in the production of Indian corn, the number of hogs packed in the West now exceeds an annual average of 5,000,000, taking the past five years, compared with 2,200,000, the annual average for the five years 1857-61.

The temptation to the prophetic soul to project imagination into the future, and conjure up a vision of ten years hence, is almost irresistible. The proportion sum looks so easy.

If 45 million men produce 50 million quarters wheat, 160 million quarters corn, $5\frac{1}{4}$ million bales of cotton, in 1878, what will 55 million of the same men produce in 1888?

The export of meat is still in its infancy. The State of Texas alone is capable of producing sufficient for all the consumption of Great Britain, and hundreds of emigrants are pouring in to that great State every day. The difficulties of carriage are almost certain to be surmounted by science. I have mentioned the production of only three great staples of export; but the money value of the hay crop in the United States is really greater than that of the cotton crop. There are almost as many quarters of oats produced as of wheat; there is rye, and petroleum, and fruits in an abundance we can scarcely realise. Surely it is a land teeming with corn, and wine, and oil, and cotton; with every kind of animal, vegetable, and mineral wealth, and anything may be predicted of it. "Among all forms of mistake," says George Eliot, "prophecy is the most gratuitous." "Man must always carry a threatening shadow under the full sunshine." And there are, and are always likely to be, plenty of shadows hanging over the human element in America. The widespread political corruption,[1] though probably not so deep-seated as in Russia to-day, or more noxious than in England 150 years ago, is a malignant disease that may easily have a fatal termination unless it is arrested in time. Its causes are multitudinous enough and subtle enough, I imagine, to elude the observation of those quick-witted, but perhaps not always deep-witted, critics who wish to found thereon a destructive charge against the republican form of government. The charge, as we see, may be equally well levelled against an autocracy, or against a monarchy with such very limited popular representation as existed in Walpole's time. And evidences are not wanting of great improvement in the United States compared with the state of things existing five or six years ago. But the reform must be determined, and a new departure must be taken, before the greatest things can be predicted of the future. In recording achievements we

---

[1] See an interesting article by Hon. John Jay on "Civil Service Reform," October – November number of 'North American Review.'

are on safer ground. "Things won are done." The prosaic fact remains that the exports from America, for the year ending 30th June last, amounted to £145,000,000, or more than double the amount of any year before the war; while the *increase* in exports of grain alone amounted to £22,000,000, and of provisions to £19,000,000, compared with 1868.

Our exports from Great Britain have increased at times with marvellous rapidity, but I do not think that we ever accomplished the feat of doubling them in so short a period as sixteen years. In America's case it has no doubt partly been a consequence of excessive borrowing; but looking to the fact that four of those years were occupied with an internecine civil war, and the liberation of four or five million slaves, on whose labour the production of cotton—the most valuable article of export—mainly depended, it is an astonishing result. If Professor Cairnes had lived, he would have seen during the last three years the exports from America exceeding the imports by £100,000,000. The effect on the exchanges has been to enable the country to keep all its own production of gold;

and the Government, on this 1st January, will have an ample coin reserve for the resumption of specie payments. Another effect has been that a large mass of securities has been taken back, so that President Hayes was recently able to say: " A few years ago the Government bonds were largely held in foreign countries. It is estimated that in 1871 from £160,000,000 to £200,000,000 were held abroad, and there was then paid from £10,000,000 to £12,000,000 annually to Europe for interest alone. Now it is estimated that five-sixths of them are held in the United States, and only one-sixth abroad. Instead of paying to foreigners £10,000,000, we now pay them only about £2,400,000 or £3,000,000 a-year; and the interest on our debt is mainly paid to our own citizens." The principal of the debt has been reduced by £160,000,000, and the annual interest by about £10,000,000 a-year, owing to the reduction of capital and refunding at reduced rates of interest.

It is probable that the accumulation of capital will now proceed at an unprecedented rate in America. The savings banks' returns are very remarkable. In the New England

States alone, out of a population of 3,500,000 persons, there were, in 1876, 1,223,000 deposit accounts open, with £64,000,000 deposited. It is true that these institutions are used by others than the poorer classes. A capitalist, by putting 1000 dollars in each of half-a-dozen names, may have 6000 dollars in one bank, for the sake of the 5 or 6 per cent interest paid. But making allowance for this, the statement is still marvellous, for the great mass of the savings really belongs to the workers, not to the capitalists as a class.

Three things are necessary to material progress and prosperity in such a country as America — and we may frankly include a country nearer home — capital, labour, and thrift. The experience of the past five years has taught men there to labour more and spend less on luxuries. The gambling element has been very much weeded out of business. The characteristic attributes of the real American masses are thrift and "invention ever new." I use "thrift" in the sense that they are not wastrels. They live more comfortably and generously than any other people in the world, but they spend nothing like the amount in drink that the English people spend. Their general extravagance under the influence of the war fever and irredeemable paper was, I am inclined to think and hope, a parasitic growth that has been lopped off. It is a country where no man is, from the necessity of his position, hopelessly cut off from his chance of the best. It is emphatically a land of "equality of conditions." Behind all is the wide West, with any quantity of excellent unimproved land still to be bought at three and a half dollars (15s.) per acre. This suits all pockets. The man with capital can do well by breaking the lands up and renting them; the labourer, with any energy and work in him, can soon lease a farm of 160 acres for himself, and finally own it.

In these Western States there seems an issue for the agricultural labour difficulties of other countries. A bright future can scarcely be hoped for farmers or labourers, either on the continent of Europe, so long as the great standing armies are maintained, or in England whilst our very limited quantity of land is kept at an altogether artificial price by the action of laws which induce the plutocracy to invest in it, regardless of return of interest, for the sake of social importance and enjoyment of sport, and where none of the workers on the soil—farmers or labourers—can look forward to its ownership. The extraordinary productiveness and facilities for communication with markets give the agriculturists far better chances in America than anywhere else. Throughout all the recent hard times, no man able and willing to work on a farm has ever been badly off. There has always been a demand for such labourers in excess of the supply, and at no diminution of wages—looking at wages in the only true sense of their purchasing power.

Of course they will have their difficulties in the United States in the future as they have had them in the past. We shall no doubt very soon be hearing the cry from the West of over-production of food—a bearable evil; for transportation charges are now higher than they were (1s. per 100 lb. for grain from Chicago!), and the hard times here will abate the demand, and cause a decline in prices; and Great Britain takes nearly two-thirds of the total American exports, so that she is a large factor in all calculations of future prosperity. With dissatisfaction in the West and South there will be a much louder demand for free trade; and if I were to depart from the golden rule of not prophesying, it would be to hazard a guess that the next great agitation will be for free trade,[1] and the next great difficulty will be the silver question.

And America's action on these two questions will have a bearing, difficult to exaggerate in the potency of its effect on our future here in England. Under the existing protective tariff the import of railroad bars, for instance, amounted to only £100 this year, against £4,000,000 in 1873: this may be accounted for, however, to some extent by the growing use of steel. In 1872 the production in the United States of Bessemer steel rails was 94,000 tons. In 1877 it had increased to 432,000 tons.[2] The import of cotton manufactures was £3,000,000, against £6,000,000

[1] The M'Kinley tariff has since shown how dangerous it is to prophesy—"unless you know!" It still remains to be seen how long the United States will stand the heavy protective duties.

[2] The production of Bessemer steel last year (1891) was 4,131,000 tons in the United States, of which about 70 per cent was worked up into railway material.

in the same period. On the other hand, the exports from America of iron, steel, and the manufactures of these metals, was £1,100,000 greater this year than in 1868 : the exports of cotton manufactures have more than doubled during the past five years, and the United States now consume 22·6 per cent of the world's total production of cotton, instead of 19·1 per cent before the war. But considering all the outcry that has recently been made about the export of American manufactures, I confess I am surprised to find that this year they only amount after all to 5 per cent of the total exports of merchandise—£7,000,000 out of £145,000,000. Without entering the tempting field of controversy between free trade and protection, it may be surmised that the protectionists in America will shortly be drawing a striking parallel between their own regained prosperity (if it lasts !) and the existing state of things in Great Britain under free trade, than which nothing could well be more deplorable. But these selected parallels are not very useful : inconvenient facts so often come immediately to refute all the conclusions arrived at. There can be little doubt that if the consumers choose to pay more for inferior goods of native manufacture, America is capable of producing almost all that her inhabitants require. And this is especially true of iron and cotton goods. How long will the West and South consent to this? In the existing conditions of the world a bad state of trade in one great country immediately affects all other countries; and if things go from bad to worse here, the continuity of improvement in America may be very rudely interrupted. It is very certain that if we are kept out of markets for our manufactures, we cannot spend the same amount of money on raw products. For the last five years we have had not only the old protective or prohibitive duties against us, but also that economy in consumption which we have seen followed the pricking of the financial balloon. It may, I think, be safely predicted that America will not go on for ever wearing her old shoes. There is still almost infinite capacity for railroad extension; and new roads, built with decent honesty at the present excessively low prices of iron, steel, and materials generally, are almost certain to pay very handsomely in time. Capital is yet timid—naturally, poor thing, after recent experiences!—but the go-ahead nature is certain to prevail in the end. And just as America's bad time started the ball for the rest of the world, so now that she has been through the unpleasant process of liquidation, it is likely that her good time will again start the ball in the opposite direction. We have probably a good deal of liquidation to get through in England before we are purged of our troubles; but if the American tariff be speedily altered, we may perhaps be found with our loins girt, and in a better frame of mind for solid work and real business than we have been in for years. We, too, have had our period of demoralisation. After the Foreign Loans Committee and the City of Glasgow Bank, we shall never more be able to throw stones at our commercial neighbours, but we may do something much more useful: we may make our work more perfect. There is an ancient proverb—(Russian, I believe)—"If every man would only keep his own doorstep swept, how clean the town would be!" Instead of those on the "upper plane" always falling foul of the working men's shortcomings, let them—

the business men among them especially—consider a little what example they set. Let them consider that almost all the worst kinds of shame have their roots in extravagance, whether of employer or of workman, of man or of woman. There is something too much of this in the latest developments of our commercial life. But this may be a passing phase. We may reform it altogether. One thing is certain, namely, that all gain of *real* wealth in America *must* be of advantage to England; and it will surely be the first sign of impending decadence if the business men of this country, instead of putting their shoulders to the wheel to carry their chariot over all obstructions, content themselves with cherishing a vindictive feeling to rivals—

> "Bear, like the Turk, no brother near the throne,
> View him with scornful yet with jealous eyes,
> And hate for arts that caused themselves to rise."

But I have left myself no space for the silver question. Indeed I should not have made so bold as to refer to it, but that one point may be worth keeping in mind in regard to America. If it be admitted that the demonetisation of silver in Europe has essentially been an immense measure of contraction of the former circulating medium, with the consequent great inconvenience of a general fall in prices as measured in gold (the result of which may, perhaps, go a long way to account for the existing wretched state of trade throughout the world), it is open to question whether, after all, Europe may not have eventually to seek an understanding with America, to endeavour to fix a relation between the value of gold and silver coins all the world over. This might help to lift us out of a great difficulty in India. Therefore let us not judge too hastily in this matter. The last word has not been said yet about silver, the Paris Conference notwithstanding.

THE FUTURE OF FOOD.[1]

AFTER the first flush of satisfaction over Mr Bear's consoling essay on 'The British Farmer and his Competitors' has died away, it may be useful to ascertain what the interesting little book has really contributed towards a solution of our farmers' difficulties. With the conclusion no one, I suppose, will find fault, "that, whatever else Parliament does for the benefit of agriculture, or leaves undone, there is one thing needful above all others — a system of land tenure based upon just and enlightened laws." There will perhaps be a difference of opinion between landowners and farmers as to what laws are just and enlightened, but there is more than one

[1] Contemporary Review, December 1888.

allusion scattered through the volume, as, for instance, on page 140—" The enormous tax levied on the people of the world by those who have got possession of the land, and are so able to appropriate a very large proportion of the earnings of every community, especially in cities and towns, is one great cause of the depressed condition of the people everywhere"—which points to sufficiently radical alterations. Further, there is the excellent recommendation of the extension of co-operation by farmers, both for the purchase of what they require and for the disposal of what they have to sell. That is a suggestion at once business-like and to the point; and perhaps it would be demanding too much from any gentleman writing in this year of grace 1888, to expect him to refrain from the remark that he "cannot conceive of any more legitimate use of public money than the devotion of a moderate sum" to the purposes which he has particularly in view. Clearly, as Sir William Harcourt has said, "we are all Socialists now." It is possible to sum up Mr Bear's positive beliefs in a sentence—Reduction of rents (where not already sufficiently conceded); security for farmers' capital; reduced railway rates; co-operation in buying and selling; and better education in agriculture. Now it is obvious that none of these things can, or will, be done in a hurry. It is doubtful whether that part of the programme which is dependent on legislation will ever be seriously attempted so long as a Conservative Government is in power, and, thanks to our friends the Liberal Unionists, there is no great likelihood of a change before 1892 or thereabouts. But after the last thirteen years of bad times, another four or five years without material alteration of conditions for the better is a serious outlook for our agricultural interests.

The Report of the Royal Commission on Depression of Trade estimated the capitalised loss of income by owners of agricultural land and their tenants in Great Britain at £740,000,000 in 1885, compared with ten years before. If that was the loss in 1885, what must it be to-day? Again, in the ten years from 1871 to 1881, the percentage of the whole population supported by agriculture decreased from 17 per cent to less than 14 per cent, and the next census for 1891 will certainly show a considerable further reduction. When we remember that thirty years ago at least 24 per cent were so supported, and when we stand face to face here in London with this most menacing increase of our urban population at the expense of our rural population, in a country which is admittedly so peculiarly well fitted for agricultural pursuits as Great Britain, it must make the boldest hold his breath. Fortunately for our peace of mind, it is difficult for us to realise—it is impossible for us to have an ever vivid consciousness of—our terrible and growing dependence on the world outside for the daily bread of our 38,000,000 of people. If we were not gifted with a plentiful lack of imagination, we should not sleep well o' nights. It would be like "feeling the squirrel's heart beat," and would end in the wrecking of our nervous systems. But the grim hard fact is always there, and every day it becomes more and more painfully obtrusive. It is therefore very natural that any hopeful and consoling view such as Mr Bear's is grasped at with avidity, and it is perhaps an ungracious task to look at it too critically. But in this, as in all other things, the only important point is to get at the truth, and not to nurse delusions. Ignorance of what is going on in the world outside this little island has been one of the most fruitful sources of our agricultural troubles. Any reasonably well-informed man could have predicted them with almost absolute certainty. That I may not be accused of prophesying after the event, I take the liberty of quoting a couple of sentences I wrote in 1878 on the future of American competition : [1]—

"The temptation to the prophetic soul to project imagination into the future, and conjure up a vision of ten years hence, is almost irresistible. The proportion sum looks so easy. If 45 million men produce 50 million quarters wheat, 160 million quarters corn, $5\frac{1}{4}$ million bales of cotton, in 1878, what will 55 million of the same men produce in 1888? The export of meat is still in its infancy. The difficulties of carriage are almost certain to be surmounted by science. I have mentioned the production of only three great staples of export; but the money value of the hay crop

[1] "America Rediviva," 'Macmillan's Magazine,' January 1879. See preceding paper.

THE FUTURE OF FOOD. 241

in the United States is really greater than that of the cotton crop. There are almost as many quarters of oats produced as of wheat: there is rye, and there are fruits in an abundance we can scarcely realise. . . . A bright future can scarcely be hoped for farmers or labourers, either on the continent of Europe, so long as the great standing armies are maintained, or in England whilst our very limited quantity of land is kept at an altogether artificial price by the action of laws which induce the plutocracy to invest in it, regardless of return of interest, for the sake of social importance and enjoyment of sport, and where none of the workers on the soil—farmers or labourers—can look forward to its ownership."

Now while, of course, it cannot be seriously attempted to work out such a complicated problem as agricultural returns by simple proportion, it is curious to note how the figures result. It was a mistake to assume in 1878 that the population of the United States would amount to only 55 million in 1888, for, as a matter of fact, it is to-day nearer 62 million. But, taking the population as 60 million in

Q

1887, the proportions would work out as follows :—

	Production ought to have been.	Actual Production.
Wheat	66 million qrs.	57 million qrs. in 1887
Indian corn	213 " "	222 " " av. 1885-88
Oats	60 " "	78 " " in 1887
Cotton	6½ " bales	7 " bales in 1887-88

Speaking roughly, the value of a quarter of Indian corn is little more than half the value of a quarter of wheat, and the value of a quarter of oats a little less than half the value of a quarter of wheat at the prices of to-day; so that the gain in the proportion of the two former cereals is much greater than the loss in the proportion of wheat—not to mention the gain of £5,000,000 in the value of the extra half-million bales of cotton. As a standard of comparison, we can add up the production of these three cereal crops in America, and we shall find that they amount to 357 million quarters, whereas the production of *all* the corn crops in the United Kingdom amounts to less than 35 million quarters. It may be added that the corn crop of 1888 just harvested is the largest ever produced in

America.[1] The reason I wish to dwell on these figures is, that it is more than doubtful whether the British agriculturist has even yet appreciated to its full extent the potency of the North American continent as the supreme factor in the future of his business, notwithstanding all that has been written on the subject. This is partly owing to his not having realised what has been done, and what is being done, in the extension of American railroads, and partly to an unfortunately worded or an unfortunately misunderstood axiom of his leaders. When Messrs Read and Pell visited the United States as Assistant Commissioners to the Royal Commission on Agriculture in 1880, they stated that 42s. per quarter was the minimum price at which the general run of American producers could sell wheat in London with profit. They may have been

---

[1] In 1891 the aggregate of all the cereal crops in the United States taken together shows the largest production ever recorded; and the yield per acre is also the largest.

The wheat crop comes up to	76 million quarters.
The Indian corn crop to	257 ,, ,,
The oat crop to	92 ,, ,,

So that the production of wheat is now more than the proportion I calculated in 1878, and Indian corn and oats very much more.

right, or they may have been wrong, in this calculation; but, as a matter of fact, the average price of wheat in London for the ten years from 1879 to 1888 has been under 40s. per quarter; and during the three years of lowest prices—1885 to 1887—when the average was only 32s. 1d. per quarter, the United States sent us 30 million quarters, or considerably more than half—say 57 per cent—of our total imports. Now undoubtedly the effect of such a statement as Messrs Read and Pell's on the British farmer was to induce him to believe that he was pretty safe never to see wheat below 42s. for any considerable period.[1] Whereas for the last six years he has never seen the price *up* to 42s., and has seen it as low as 31s., the average of the year 1886. Ten years is a very long period for the average price of a main article of production to be selling 5 per cent below its supposed minimum, and the consequences of such mistakes are disastrous. The safest plan surely is to distrust all calculations where one of the most important factors—the price of

[1] The average price of wheat in Great Britain for 1891 was 37s. per quarter. It is now under 30s. per quarter (1892).

carriage—is and must always remain an uncertain and an unknown quantity. For instance, if any wise man had told us in America in 1870 that eight years later (in 1878) we should have been able to transport 100 lb. of wheat from Chicago to New York for 6d., we should have looked on the supposition as incredible.

With the extension of the means for transportation and the discoveries science is making every day, it is practically impossible to say what rates of freight may decline to. Similarly, all anticipations that countries with large wheat-fields will cease sending wheat because somebody is ready to prove that it leaves a loss, should be distrusted. Ever since I entered the American trade in 1857, I have always been told that farmers were making losses, and that it was calculably impossible to send grain from such and such a point in the West at a profit. The only answer is, that they have always kept on sending it ever in greater and greater volume, and, comparing the total value of farms between one census period and another in the United States, we do not find any record of ruin.

£1,852,000,000 in 1870 against £2,000,000,000 in 1880, for instance. Mr Bear quotes Mr Bookwalter, who says :—

"The real advantage heretofore possessed by the American agriculturist, cheap lands (the rapid rise of which, in recent years, and not the profits of farming, being the real source of his present wealth) and natural fertility, are rapidly disappearing; and unless his Government removes the cause which operates to artificially increase cost of production, the English farmer will have year by year less cause to fear serious competition from America."

Now everything, of course, depends on the interpretation of the word "rapidly." If the present generation of English farmers expect during their lifetime to see cheap lands disappearing in the United States and Canada—lands eminently fitted for growing wheat—I think they will be disappointed. So far from anticipating that they have less to fear from American competition in the future than in the past, they will be better advised to believe that American competition is still in its infancy.

Mr Bookwalter's view, and the whole tone of Mr Bear's little book, remind me of the man who, in 1837-40, comforted the old coach-owners and the inns on the road by saying that sooner or later those infernal railroads would all burst up. Well, 1848 came, and they did burst up, but all the Queen's horses and all the Queen's men couldn't put the old coaches on the road again. The difference between the American system and conditions of agriculture compared with the British is the difference between railroads and coaches. The latter must suffer in the competition. Mr Bear quotes a passage from Dornbusch, which it is well to reflect on : *"Although cereal production has not been checked in Russia, wheat-growing does not pay."* He might have added that, although wheat-growing may not pay, wheat-growing will not be seriously checked on the North American continent. Now, is there any warrant for saying this? There is the warrant of experience.

Wherever extension of railroads takes place in the new States and territories of the American continent — or anywhere else, for that matter, where there is virgin soil—there wheat-growing is bound to increase. Let us, then, consider for a moment what has been done in this direction during the last ten years. Since 1878 the United States have built 80,000 miles of new railroad—of which 20,000 have been built in the last eighteen months—a bit of industrial work wholly unparalleled in the history of the world. It is difficult to know how to compare it with anything of the same sort elsewhere, for when we come to contrast the figures of mileage in one country with those in another, we are met with difficulties in the calculation of double tracks, sidings, and other matters, which can only be adjusted by experts. But we can compare one period with another in the same country with better chance of enlightenment, because the variations from accuracy will be more or less constant. There cannot then be a doubt, I think, that on December 31 of this year there will be nearly 160,000 miles of railroad open for traffic, compared with 80,000 ten years ago; and the gross receipts last year (1887-88) amounted to £187,000,000, compared, for instance, with gross receipts of about £105,000,000 from all the railways in the whole British Empire—

including India, Canada, Australia, and all our other colonies. Or, to put the case in a still more striking way, the United States, with sixty million inhabitants, took about the same gross receipts as Great Britain, France, Germany, and Russia in Europe combined, with 210 million inhabitants, took from all their railroads. Assuming £5000 per mile as a low actual cost for building and equipping these new lines, the expenditure of hard cash must have amounted to £400,000,000 in the last ten years—a sum equal to more than half our National Debt—and the nominal value of securities issued against them is probably a good deal over £800,000,000. Now, railways are the heavy artillery in modern industrial warfare, and English farmers will be better occupied in making themselves acquainted with what is being done in this direction than in laying the flattering unction to their souls that American competition is on the wane. What they should particularly bear in mind is, that out of the total 13,000 miles built last year, 9000 miles are west of the Missouri river—the State of Kansas alone having 2100 miles of new lines.

To most of us the State of Kansas, and all the country west, north-west, and south-west of it, is merely a geographical expression; but if we look at the map we shall find that the centre of it is, roughly speaking, exactly midway between the Atlantic and the Pacific Oceans. There are five magnificent States and territories—Colorado, Nebraska, Dakota, Montana, and Wyoming, with a combined acreage equal to that of Great Britain, France, Germany, Holland, and Belgium together—being opened up to the west and north-west, and a country of about equal extent on the south-west, in Texas, New Mexico, and Arizona. The process of development is a continuous tapping of new and virgin sources of supply over an area equal to the whole of Europe, bar Russia, in these eight States and territories, whose total population, all told, does not yet amount to the population of London. The density is at present about 4 to the square mile, against 520 per square mile in Belgium, for instance. It will take a long time yet before cheap lands disappear in these regions—which only want a system of irrigation to make them immensely productive—

THE FUTURE OF FOOD. 251

not to mention the Dominion of Canada. Looking to the gigantic scale on which agricultural operations are conducted, and on which railroads are built on the other side of the Atlantic, I think it is a bold prognostication to anticipate any material decrease in the production of wheat, even when prices are below 42s. per quarter in London. If prices rise above that point we can be deluged with quantity. The increase is so sudden. For instance, the average production of wheat for the five years 1870-75 in the United States was 33 million quarters. In 1878 it had risen to 50 million quarters, increasing to an average of about 56 million quarters during the last four years, when the price has averaged just 33s. per quarter in London. Deducting the export of those four years from the production, leaves about 40 million quarters as the average annual consumption of wheat in America. If the production keeps up to 56 million quarters, there will remain a large excess for export even with increasing population. But when wheat is below 40s., there are many chances of a rise, against very few chances of a fall. We live with the daily prospect of a great European war constantly before us, and in that event the price of wheat might easily be doubled in a few weeks. That dreaded disaster may be on us at any moment, and without warning. Looking to these possibilities of a great rise in the price of wheat, and no great risk of a fall under 35s. to 40s., the acreage planted over the world will not materially diminish yet. And, in passing, I must allude to what appears to me to be a strange tone in a book issued under the auspices of the Cobden Club. Mr Bear seems rather to *hope* for a rise in the price of wheat. I should have thought genuine and thorough-going free-traders would have wished to see wheat down to 22s. rather than up to 42s. per quarter. I cannot understand on what theory of free trade any true believer can object to wheat or sugar declining to the lowest possible prices. Surely in both cases the old argument remains true, that the gain to the mass of the community, who are consumers, is of more consequence than the loss to the small class of landlords or sugar-producers. I say this rather from the point of view of the Cobden

Club. From another point of view it may be said that we are better not to be under bondage to dogmas—whether the dogma be free trade or another. When we look at the world around us, we do not see success invariably and inevitably attending either the free trade nations or the protectionists. In the last fifteen years certainly, the nations that have been gaining most, relatively speaking, in the race for wealth and commercial supremacy, are the Americans and the Germans. They are both protectionists, and both nations are surely characterised by a very vigorous intelligence, an unprecedented universality of education, a keen commercial spirit, and uncommonly sharp eyes to their own interests. Their success may either be in consequence of, or in spite of, what we may consider to be their fiscal heresies. I do not presume to say. But is it not just conceivable that the effect of mere fiscal arrangements may very easily be grossly exaggerated, and that success rather follows *character?* The race is to the strong, to the intelligent, to the hardest working, to the best educated peoples. To know what they want, and to see that they get it, is the first essential for any people. The little more or the little less of duties (except on food in England, under our existing conditions!) is a detail—no doubt an important detail—but, after all, the duties go out of one pocket into another in the same country. Free trade seems to me, if I may say so, to be the only ultimate sensible solution all the world over; but meantime almost every great country except England thinks differently, and it does not appear that they are all prospering less, relatively speaking. No doubt it is true that, owing to America's protective policy, her mercantile marine has been swept from the seas. But notwithstanding their soreness on the subject, the Americans may very well console themselves with the reflection that the same country cannot do everything at the same time. Sentiment apart, shipowning is a question of profit—*or loss*. If the Americans had built steamers to share in the profits (?) of the last few years, it would indeed have been an attempt "to tak' the breeks aff a Hielandman." There may have been much glory to England, but there has been very little profit, owing to the unprecedented lowness of freights. The practical question arises, " Is shipowning the most desirable business that Americans can undertake at present?" They have to consider whether the capital of their country is not much more profitably employed in manufacturing steel and iron rails, locomotives, and all the other requisites for railroad transportation (which, by the way, protective duties have enabled them to do with very signal success, not only as regards the extraordinary improvement in the quality of the articles in the last few years, but also in securing diversified employment for hundreds of thousands of workmen who become the farmers' best customers), and thus completing the iron ways within their own borders, which go on for ever, make available the produce of every inch of land they traverse, and increase in value every year. Steamers, on the other hand, are constantly depreciating, and become valueless after a certain—and a very limited—number of years, having spent the best part of their lives in ploughing that old ocean on which they can leave no track, nor improve its saleable value! Unquestionably the world must have an effective service of steamers, and, if the necessity ever arises, the Americans may be depended on to supply them quickly; but in the meantime the competition in Great Britain, supplemented by the bounty-fostered efforts of other nations, leaves no cause of complaint either as to efficiency or cheapness of carriage. In fact, this cheapness of freights is one of the main causes of our farmers' difficulties. For it is not only in the United States that we see this extraordinary activity in railroad-building. The same thing is going on at a great rate, though on a less gigantic scale, in Canada and the Argentine Republic. Mr Bear speaks with a good deal of contempt of the pretensions of these countries as wheat-growers. It may be admitted that they have been perhaps a little premature in announcing themselves as "the future granaries of the world." But Mr Bear should not be in a hurry to conclude that, because such countries may actually be importers of wheat to-day, they may not be very large exporters in an uncommonly short space of time. Any middle-aged man can remember the day when both California and Australia were importers of wheat and flour. The British farmer should make careful note of the immense sums now being borrowed in this country for railroad-building in South America. Within the last few months the Argentine Republic has granted concessions, with guarantee of interest, to new railroads to the extent of forty millions sterling—an enormous outlay for such a country, as the London money market is now learning to its cost.[1] In Canada, again, we have not by any means yet had time to see the effect of the opening of the Canadian Pacific Railroad on the wheat-fields it traverses, particularly in the Saskatchewan Valley. Early frosts may have lessened the production this year, but there may be no early frost next year. Unless all accounts are false, we must certainly look for a great increase in the production of wheat from these regions, whatever the price may be in London. When we turn to India, I see no reason to anticipate a reduction in the

[1] The crisis of 1890—which happened two years after this paper was written—was mainly attributable to these Argentine loans.

bonus on exportations from any sustained rise in the value of silver. Mr Bear has explained very lucidly how, when the value of the pound sterling increases in rupees (whilst there is not a corresponding increase in the rupee price of commodities), exportations are stimulated. What reason is there to believe that such a process is likely to be arrested, looking to the production and the existing stocks of silver in the world? The only action likely to arrest it would be the world becoming bimetallist, and that seems to be a long way off. It is very difficult to express any positive opinion about the effect of the depreciation of the rouble in respect of the exports from Russia; but it may safely be said about any backward, slow-moving country, where banking accommodation is in its infancy, and information does not travel rapidly, that the depreciation in the value of the currency always outruns the appreciation in the price of commodities, and so exportation is stimulated. The British farmer may have to contend with the same difficulty before very long in America, because it is scarcely possible that the United States can

THE FUTURE OF FOOD. 259

continue to coin silver at the present rate, and yet remain on a gold basis. Here, again, the depreciation in the value of the dollar would probably take place a little quicker than the appreciation in the dollar value of wheat. But with American lucidity of thought, and the extraordinary development of banking facilities, prices would soon equalise themselves. The risk, however, is an additional one to be taken into consideration by our farmers.

And now I wish to come to a point a little larger than the mere production of wheat, which is, after all, only one item—although so large a one—in agriculture. What can we reasonably suppose will be the effect of the expenditure within the last few years of these hundreds of millions sterling on new railroads running through virgin soils, whose fee-simple can still be acquired for an old song, in comparison with the price of land in England? What are the millions of people now settling on these lands going to do with their land, their labour, and their railways? The answer is obvious. They are all going to *produce*, in ever greater and greater quantity, and, so long as our ports are open, they are going to send us their productions. One gets a little tired of the argument about farming not paying in America. At the risk of becoming wearisome, let me just give these figures from that played-out old State, Massachusetts :—

Total value of agricultural property—	
In 1885	£43,000,000
In 1875	37,000,000
Number of persons engaged in agriculture—	
In 1885	78,000
In 1875 . .	71,000

The conclusion at which the Census Commissioner arrives is, that while Massachusetts is not a great farming State, and does not compare with the great Western States in the great staple products of the soil, it has succeeded in gradually replacing these products by minor crops, which have, nevertheless, proved to be more remunerative, and that the increasing value of these crops offers great encouragement to the further development of the farming interests of the commonwealth. Here, again, is American lucidity of thought. They change quickly to meet changed circumstances. In Massachusetts, dairy products—

hay, straw, fodder, and vegetables—account for more than five-eighths of the total agricultural production. That can only be quickly effected in a land where the occupier is the owner, and is trammelled by no burdensome conditions in leases. I ask again, What are all these millions of emigrants to the Far West of America, to Canada, to the Argentine Republic, going to do with themselves and their land? No man can eat more than his three or four square meals a-day. An ever-growing surplus of food *must* come to us. With our antiquated system of land tenure, the contest between us and these new countries in the production of food is like the contest between great commercial companies and small shopkeepers. Unless we reform our agricultural system it means ruin. A great European war might stave it off for a time. But, of course, looking to the interests of the whole country, such a cure would be a great deal worse than the disease. England would probably herself be involved sooner or later, and that would indeed be a case of burning our house down to roast our pig. From this point of view, to whatever party we belong, we can have but one policy, and that is to bring our navy up to a proper strength for its multifarious and most portentous duties. It is a simple principle of fire insurance, and whoever neglects that duty will, sooner or later, incur unparalleled national resentment. But supposing there is no war, what warrant have we for supposing that the prices of food will be higher? I cannot see any valid reason: and the *lower* prices are the better,—we ought all to be pleased except the landowners and the farmers. What a curious commentary it is on the danger of prophecy, to consider that in this year 1888, when Mr Malthus would have proved to us that population was bound to have outrun the means of subsistence, the fact is that the means of subsistence were never in greater abundance, in proportion to the population, than they are in England to-day. Taking the British colonies, the North American continent, and the Argentine Republic, there are to-day 360 million head of cattle, sheep, and pigs, which were practically represented by zero when Mr Malthus published his first edition. With the extension of transportation facilities, all these vast flocks and herds will sooner or later be available for the meat-supply of England. And there is this further consideration, that if we look at the Western World as a whole, we shall find that a great deal more than half of it is suffering from under-population in a greater degree than the remaining part is suffering from over-population. Looking to the way in which space has been, and is being, annihilated, I believe it to be strictly true to say that every averagely healthy, strong child of the Anglo-Saxon race, born free from inherited intemperance, and fitted by suitable education for any kind of work, is a distinct gain, instead of a loss, in the struggle for existence, because every such child will be able to produce more than it can consume. The labour markets of two continents—the American and the Australasian—are contending for his or her services. There is no prospect of lack of subsistence in these new worlds for hundreds of millions of people who are physically able for, and are morally not afraid of or disinclined to, *rough* work. The pressing national question for us in England is how to obtain this right sort of people, and how to prevent deterioration in quality.

This is really a more practicable end to aim at than a diminution in their *quantity*. The difficulty and danger of over-population nowadays arises precisely amongst that class of helpless, hopeless ones who will be the last to apply any moral self-restraint, and it would be difficult to instance a nation whose population is at a standstill or diminishing in numbers which is free from *la misère*. We have to borrow the very term from France to get the exact *nuance* of meaning, and it certainly cannot be asserted that population in France is increasing in a threatening manner. We hear nothing now but complaints of the reverse, and that the nation is consequently falling into a state of decadence. How, then, are we to better the quality of our people? Clearly, first of all, by re-marrying the people to the land—if that be possible. Let us hope, too, that the State or the municipalities will take up energetically the great questions of systematic emigration, technical education, housing, draining, lighting, open-air spaces, baths and wash-houses, gymnasia, and all the other means for making the mass of the people's lives brighter and better. For, after all, they — the masses — *are* "the State." The food-supply may then be left to take care of itself.

Mem., 1892.—Lord Salisbury is now also to be reckoned among the prophets. He sees that the only salvation for English agriculture is to increase the number of holdings; and as Mr Arthur Balfour in his Irish Land Bill has introduced the principle of State socialism in its most flagrant form, it is difficult to see the arguments that will be adduced on the other side when it is proposed to apply the same principles to England. Some of us may begin to think that we are too much "all Socialists now." With the two parties competing against one another in the same direction there will be no cog on the wheels, and we may soon have to bewail as our greatest political misfortune that there is no real Conservative party in this country.

SOCIAL NEW YORK.[1]

THE outward appearance of the city of New York has been so often described that it is tolerably well known to English readers. The fine bay, with its white sails and the usually clear blue sky overhead, forming so great a contrast to the Mersey, gives at once to the American-bound traveller a comfortable sense of breadth and cheeriness. There is nothing dull to look at; nothing hopeless; nothing hateful in ugliness and gloom. And Broadway, although we may find it much narrower

[1] Macmillan's Magazine, June 1872. It must be remembered that this little paper was written twenty years ago, and I am told that things have changed very much socially in New York, as they have done in England. They have been Anglicising their ideas, whilst we have been Americanising ours. Such is life.

than we imagined, and very disappointing in the incongruity and tastelessness of its architecture (with the wretched flagstaffs of different sizes on every roof, and flaunting signs stuck up at every door-post), has still an attraction from the novelty and the scale of many of its buildings; and there is a display of wealth and bustling eager activity about the street that give it a character of its own. Fifth Avenue, too, with its handsome brown stone houses, and the trees bordering the pavement in their fresh green, is a sight to please the eye. It is a sort of street we have not been accustomed to. It is typically American. It would be difficult to match its three miles in comfort and sightliness. It is already built out to the Central Park, the great pride and glory of New Yorkers. Within the last ten or twelve years this park has been formed out of an absolute wilderness of rock. The roads in it are perfect. The turf is admirably kept, and no English lawn can look brighter or greener than it does in spring. Fine timber there is none, and never can be, owing to the want of depth of soil, but flowering shrubs and small trees there are in abundance, with several artificial lakes very picturesquely laid out; and whether in springtime in its freshness, or in the fall, when autumn's "fiery finger" is laid among the leaves, the Park has a bright, pleasant appearance, with its crowds of well-dressed people walking about, and the numerous "waggons" with fast-trotting horses.

When the ordinary tourist, without letters of introduction, asks what more there is to be seen in this the third largest city in the civilised world, it must be difficult to direct him. There are one or two collections of modern pictures in private houses open to view, which might interest him for half an hour. If addicted to education or charitable institutions, he can occupy some time and receive much valuable information from visiting the schools and other buildings devoted to these purposes. If commercially inclined, the shipping and the "Bulls and Bears" in Wall Street will claim attention; but at the end of three or four days he must join in the general verdict of travellers, which has not been favourable to New York. Now, although it must be admitted that, as a metropolis, it is very deficient in objects of general interest, the ground on which it may claim both attention and study has scarcely been travelled over by any foreigner. That ground is the interior life— the social life of the city. For in their social as well as in their political innovations Americans exhibit the same tendency towards an equality of conditions. In both cases the general result is a wonderful average of content with less of extraordinary eminence in culture and refinement than may be found among the few in such a country as England, but with a much wider diffusion of apparent happiness among the many.

The same Englishman who devoutly thanks Heaven that he does not live in a land where gentlemen take no part in the government, and where such frauds can be perpetrated as have recently come to light in New York city administration, will return thanks with equal fervour that his wife and daughters do not squander his substance in millinery, nor their own time in frivolities. Scarcely, perhaps, giving due weight to the fact that however deplorable certain blemishes may be in the practical working of these American institutions, the country, whether by aid of them or in spite of them, thrives—and in the one case the spectacle is presented of forty millions of the best educated, the best fed, the best clothed, and the most contented people in the world; and in the other, that whatever defects may be found in the social organisation, one end, and not an unimportant one, is attained —namely, securing a very great amount of happiness for a very large number of young people, by encouraging them in constant opportunities of meeting, of getting to know one another, and of marrying. This latter feature is of special interest to us in England, for we are becoming so ultra-civilised that love-marriages are in some danger of going altogether out of existence; the prevalent and growing idea of man's real enjoyment being, apparently, to get away from petticoats. In America, on the other hand, scarcely any amusement is popular in which the presence of ladies is not *the* essential part. The "tournament of doves" languishes in New York because ladies will not go there.

Take an ordinary croquet-party, or a yachting-party, or a picnic; or, better still, take the general way in which average young gentlemen in the two countries will spend a holiday. In London, it will be a party of men to shoot, or hunt, or row, or play cricket, or whatever else it may be; it will seldom occur to them to take ladies with them as one of the elements in their pleasure-seeking. It will as little occur to the same class of men in New York not to take them. There the first thing thought of is a matron, and as many young ladies as there are gentlemen; and whether they drive out for a game of croquet and a dinner to the Four-in-Hand Club, or to see the horses in training at the Jockey Club, or steam up the noble Hudson to picnic among the Highlands, or go to some house in the country for luncheon and a dance afterwards, or down the bay in a yacht, or (if the season be winter) on a sleighing-party, the great point aimed at—the circumstance from which the chief pleasure is expected to be derived —is the association of ladies and gentlemen together. And this association, which is thus prized, esteemed, and, one may say, lived for by American men, cannot be said to be more than tolerated by Englishmen, and that not always with the best grace in the world. We see the results in the dreariness of our garden-parties, our croquet-parties, our archery-parties.

In America we find women, and especially unmarried women, holding a higher rank, relatively to men, than they do in this country. More deference is shown to them — more courtesy. They are encouraged to feel that they are the most important element in the social happiness of the men; and the consequence is, among the better, but not at all uncommon styles of girls, there is a most charming want of constraint, affectation, or mannerism. They are very little conventional or self-conscious, and the just mean is very often found where perfect freedom does not verge on forwardness, pertness, or fastness. And this is due not merely to the difference in the numerical proportion of men and women in the country, but it must also, in great part, be attributed to the independence in which American girls are brought up from their childhood. They become recognised leaders in all amusements, and are able to dictate a tone to society. For society seems to be a good deal like any other bully—a very great coward when made to feel the strong hand; and young ladies, aware of their tremendous social power when organised, cease to be satisfied with graceless inattentions from men. And is not this want of community between men and women in their interests and amusements

" . . . the little rift within the lute,
That by-and-by will make the music mute"?

And that is sad if it happens to the sweetest of all music here in England.

The prevalent English notion of New York society is that it is a perfect sink of iniquity; but bad though it may be—and its best friend could not say much for some sections of it—there is nowhere the same effrontery in vice as can be seen in London or Paris.

Another and perhaps a stronger point is that Americans are very far indeed from recognising the inherent superiority of boys over girls which is admitted without question in most English families, and which was so well satirised some years ago by 'Punch,' in the story of the schoolboy at home, asked by a visitor the number of his family, and answering, "Well, if you count the girls, we're eight. *I'm one.*" The taunt may go for what it is worth, were it not that the poor girls pay the penalty of their inferiority in a form appreciable by the dullest understanding or sensibility,—namely, in being left £20,000 where their brothers are left £200,000, if their parents are wealthy! In America they share and share alike. And all the advantages that money can buy will be lavished on the daughters, while the sons will be turned into a counting-house or lawyer's office at seventeen or eighteen years old, and will be made to work for their living, with little or no money help from their fathers. It is not therefore altogether surprising that in their own estimation young ladies on the other side of the Atlantic have, as they themselves would phrase it, a much more "lovely time" than their cousins here. From their childhood they assume the position of the greatest importance in society. When they are seven or eight years old they go to "dancing schools" or classes, where they meet boys two or three years older than themselves, and from that time forward they are thrown into constant association with the other sex.

The consequence is, that at whatever age you may see an American boy and girl together, you are never pained by that wretched *mauvaise honte* so common in England.

A college boy of fifteen or seventeen in New York will make visits to his girl-friends of thirteen or fourteen, and treat them with thorough courtesy. He will have plenty to say to them, and will say it naturally,—not in the least off his ease, and yet not as a general rule forward. It is his ambition to know many of them, to be a favourite with them, and their pursuits and amusements out of school will be in common. These boys go into society at a ridiculously early age, and are often very indifferently educated. Many of them, of course, are readers, and make up in later life for any early deficiencies; but many have an extremely low intellectual standard —being quite contented with that amount of knowledge or native smartness that will enable them to succeed in importing fancy dry goods or in selling stocks and gold in Wall Street: and yet with all that there will generally be found a "grace of courtesy" ingrained in them which makes it impossible for them to be otherwise than polite to a lady, or indeed to any other human being.

It would be absolutely impossible to find twelve American gentlemen in an omnibus on a wet day some of whom would not make room for a woman—and do it with grace, as if they had a pleasure in the doing of it. They would always prefer even that a man should come in and stand on their toes with his umbrella dripping over them, than that he should be left out in discomfort. Most of us who take occasion to travel in these not very aristocratic conveyances in London may remember to have noticed the expressions and actions of the five on each side when a lady passenger makes her appearance as No. 11 at the door — the alacrity to make room and remove her embarrassment as to which side she should choose, and the pleasant welcome given! However, we have rules and regulations as to complements which are conspicuous for their absence in New York. It is outrageous the way in which they fill their omnibuses and cars—exactly like the carts one sees in London streets filled with calves —not only with all the sitting and standing room taken up, but with men hanging on to the platforms, and that under no necessity of exceptional pressure, but as an everyday occurrence. One often hears in this country unfavourable comments on American manners, and it is true that they may often be found not altogether consonant with the highest grace or finish; but a stranger may travel "from Maine to California, and from the Great Lakes to the Gulf of Mexico," with very tolerable certainty that he will never encounter the slightest wilful impoliteness unless he himself gives occasion for it. On the other hand, he will often find excessive courtesy from rough exteriors where he might little expect it, exhibited not in waste of words but in kindness of action. Even in a California emigrant steamer, an Englishman, busy in taking care of his guns and of his bath-tub and of himself generally, may, if he has the eyes to see and the heart to understand, learn some lessons in chivalry—an accomplishment of bygone days — from these same rough Western fellows, who may have shocked his delicate sensibility by eating peas with their knives, and by chewing tobacco. Under a glaring tropical sun it will be their first business on arriving at Aspinwall to carry ashore the chairs and other movables, including babies of women in no way connected with them, helpful to get them good places in the new steamer at Panama—unmindful, till that is done, of their own comfort. Is it, then, this equality of conditions that tends to greater courtesy, greater kindliness in manner? Certainly these qualities are noticeable among American men. As for the women, they are very bewitching from their sprightliness; but they are sometimes spoilt more or less by the attentions they receive, looking upon the men merely as providers for their amusement, and they may be a little too apt to regard what they designate "having a good time" as the most important object in life; but still, as a rule, they appear to make good wives and mothers. And while they are young life certainly is made very easy to them, very joyous, as it naturally should be. Their association with the other sex is encouraged in every direction. Nothing so pleasantly surprises an English gentleman who goes to a New York ball well introduced, as to be asked by half-a-dozen fair maidens of eighteen to twenty years of age, to whom he may have been presented, to call on them any evening. As it is only in exceptional instances that their papas or mammas add to the crush in a ball-room, he is not likely to have the faintest idea who his new friends may be; but the invitation having been given in the frankest, kindest manner, he naturally takes advantage of it, and on the first occasion will probably be introduced to the parents and the rest of the family. But on all future occasions he is as likely as not to find the young lady quite alone. Not that she will deliberately so contrive it as to be alone. It would be truer to say that no one else will deliberately contrive that she should not be alone; and yet so habitual is this custom, that there will not be the smallest constraint or consciousness in her manner. She conducts herself exactly as if it was the most natural thing in the world that two young people should be alone together. Perhaps the most common form for the visit to take will be that the young lady receives her friend in an ante-room, while the rest of the family, with folding-doors open between, will be proceeding with their ordinary avocations in the adjoining room, precisely as if no foreign element were present. Each girl in the family will have her own distinct circle of acquaintance, both men and women—so that Maria's friends are possibly unknown except by sight to Julia, and papa's and mamma's friends may be quite unknown to both young ladies. In some large houses in New York, where two or three of the girls are in society, each receives her own friends in her own boudoir, where her visitor is shown up straight from the front door, and where she has her piano and her own favourite books and flowers about her. He comes and goes without seeing any other member of the family, and this unconstrained intimacy tends naturally towards matrimony.

The safety of the arrangement lies in the numbers. For the visitor going out is likely to stumble on another coming in, and the same young lady will walk or ride alone in the park with a different gentleman every day of the week, or will be seen one day perched on one of those marvellous "light waggons," with very scanty room for two on the seat, behind a pair of trotters speeded up to a "two-forty gait" (twenty-two miles an hour); the next day, alongside a different driver, on an English dog-cart with a tandem team; or a third day reclining with a third cavalier among buffalo robes in a sleigh, rattling along under the merry music of its silver bells. In whatever form the men amuse themselves, the companionship of ladies seems to be a necessity for their thorough enjoyment.

And to this may be attributed the lightness of the atmosphere of American entertainments. At a New York dinner there is certain to be a very large proportion of young married ladies and girls recently "come out," and these women are often so beautiful to look on and so coquette (without being flirts at all in the offensive sense of the word), simply so frankly ready to be admired and to be pleased, and so anxious to please, that no man can have time to realise any defects or wants. He welcomes the new sensation of seeing people thoroughly and unrestrainedly enjoying themselves in their own way. It may not be the highest way, but they are there for the purpose of enjoyment—and they do enjoy themselves, and do not consider it necessary to give themselves airs either of frigidity, gushing sentimentality, literary enthusiasm, or fastness. They are simply natural. Of course in a city of the size of New York there are numerous sets in what may be called "the best society," comprising every tone of culture or want of culture. It would not surprise you to find in an average dinner company several men unaware of the existence of well-known recent works, as for instance the 'Idyls of the King,' 'The Spanish Gypsy,' or 'The Ring and the Book.' But at the very same table you might find yourself taken up sharp by a girl in her teens if you ventured to air a doubtful knowledge of Mr Herbert Spencer's writings, or were to quote Buckle inaccurately. It would probably, however, be difficult to find anything like the number of quiet dinner-parties in New York that may be found in London, where various subjects of political, literary, or scientific interest are conversed about with considerable knowledge on the part of the talkers, and where it would be impossible for any one to circulate without a very fair acquaintance with the current literature of the day. "Shop" is the general bane of average New York dinner conversation among men.

Then there is generally a hearty desire on the part of every one to have a "good time"; and as hospitality is one of the cardinal virtues of American character, whatever your host has of best in the way of wines and cigars, is sure to be forthcoming without stint. There is none of that repression which is the cold blanket on so many English entertainments, where those who consider themselves as a little grander socially than their neighbours must always be asserting their supremacy; and where from the butcher to the baronet so many people are always striving to be what they are not, and to force themselves into the society of others whose whole end and aim in life is to avoid associating with them. In New York the lawyer, the banker, the merchant, and the broker all associate on terms of perfect equality as gentlemen; and out of business hours you may see the young broker without a shilling of fortune, but who is a gentleman, take a position in society that a millionaire banker

who may not be a gentleman would give his
ears to obtain, and never can obtain. In
England there is a very general — almost a
universal—impression or reproach that money
will do anything in New York; but we who
live in so thin a glass-house cannot afford
to throw stones. Many a railway magnate
who may have amassed a fortune—compared
with which Hudson's in his palmiest days
would have been scarcely a competence—is
as rigidly interdicted from any decent society
in New York, as Hudson was warmly welcomed in those circles which claim to call
themselves the select society of London. It
is very hard to say what does constitute the
right of *entrée* into good society in New York;
but it most certainly is not wealth alone.
There seems to be a sort of process of natural
selection of all those people who in themselves
contribute something to the general enjoyment. For in all their social gatherings enjoyment is the chiefest point considered. This
is especially noticeable in a ball-room. The
genius of the people goes out much towards
dancing. Nothing can be more perfect of its
kind than one of their assemblies at " Del-

monico's." "Delmonico's" is an institution of New York, a Swiss family of that name having for long been the chief restaurateurs of the city. They have rented a couple of the handsomest houses in Fifth Avenue, and have built a ball-room behind them, which is used not only for these public assemblies, but is very generally hired by any one wishing to give a large private ball. The suite of rooms is sufficiently handsome; and as four or five hundred people can be accommodated without crushing, there is generally room to move about and to dance. The bulk of the matronising is done by comparatively few young married ladies, each of whom will take charge of a number of girls who report themselves to her as a matter of form. It is a very pretty sight to see one of these young matrons enter the *salon bleu*, the reception-room, with half-a-dozen girls in her train, each carrying from one to half-a-dozen bouquets of exquisite flowers. They have a rare faculty for dressing well—understanding how to wear their fine things, and having in general a perception of the harmony of colours, aided by a liberality in allowance attained by a diversion of much that English fathers devote to the hunting and shooting proclivities of their sons. A ball-room presents a rich brilliant appearance, like a gay parterre of flowers. Dancing has been elevated almost into an art, and it is very rare to see either man or woman who does not dance really well. Pace and endurance are not so much cultivated in America as grace; and the whole room does not set to dancing, or rather jostling one another, at the same moment. Rows of respectable but uncalled-for papas and mammas, consuming valuable air and space, are unknown. The young girls are consequently the lords of the ascendant, and they look as if they felt it, as they are entitled to do in a ball-room.

Quadrilles and lancers are never danced, having gone out of fashion as completely as stage-coaches. Waltzes and galops alternate till twelve o'clock, when the favourite German cotillon, with its many fanciful, pretty, and graceful figures, begins and lasts till any hour in the morning. Dancing young ladies seem to be divided into two sets: one of which dances everything except, and the other nothing but, "the German."

The men having been taught dancing from their infancy, and having kept it up ever since, seem to enjoy a ball as much as the women—and the women are radiant. The universality of flower-carrying adds very much to the effectiveness of their appearance. It is extremely rare to see any lady quite bouquetless; and it is a pleasant custom and a natural one that a man should send to any woman or to many women whom he admires, or to whom he may be indebted for civilities, flowers either in baskets for their boudoirs or in bouquets to swell their triumphs at a ball. They express a sentiment as lightly as it can be expressed, without having any undue weight attached either by giver or receiver. The sending of the flowers is good for the man, in that for the moment he has thought of some one's pleasure besides his own: the receiving of them is good for the woman, because it puts her in charity with all men and women. The drawback is the want of moderation which characterises things American. The cost of a choice ball bouquet is ten or twelve dollars, so that a belle may often be seen entering a room with ten or twelve pounds sterling worth of flowers in her hands, as five bouquets will be no unusual number. As they will all be cast out next day, the waste of money is excessive, for the sentiment cannot be measured in dollars. Baskets of flowers, of course, run to much greater excess — twenty pounds or forty pounds being often paid in winter for handsome ones.

Even in their club-life the New York men seem to aim at including the other sex. They have a Four-in-Hand Club, which certainly belongs as much to the ladies as to the gentlemen, so far as regards the uses to which it is put and the pleasures derived from it. The Club-house is beautifully situated on a knoll overlooking the Hudson, some eight miles from the city, and was built for the purpose of giving dinners and dances. The view from it up and down the river is lovely, and many a pleasant ladies' dinner (always including unmarried girls) is given there in the long summer afternoons. In the winter-time, dances with thirty or forty couple, and the return home in a sleigh behind a gentleman-whip slightly exhilarated (of course by the keen frosty air), and doing his honest sixteen or eighteen miles an hour, with the moon shining out cold and clear—no "nebulous hypothesis" as we are accustomed to in this little isle—and the bright stars (much more steadfast than the driver), and the solos and the choruses accompanying the joyous ringing of the silver bells, leaves a pleasant—very pleasant—impression on the mind of him who, through the storm of the singing, may still be listening to a still small voice very near him.

Another pleasant innovation is the custom of giving theatre or opera parties. Any unmarried young lady or gentleman can select a matron and ask half-a-dozen or a dozen of their friends to go to the theatre or opera; the entertainment being generally prefaced by a dinner, or followed by a supper and an impromptu "German" at Delmonico's. You very rarely turn into any theatre in New York without seeing a party of young people enjoying themselves in this way. It is, perhaps, as pleasant a way of passing an evening as any other, to dine at half-past six and go to the opera afterwards. If unfortunate in your right and left at dinner, there is the chance of a new deal subsequently—and that again failing, there is always the piece to look at, with closed eyes, perhaps, if the light is strong ! It will be understood that the opera is a much cheaper amusement in New York than in London, and in itself inferior in fully equal proportion. In fact, there is nothing first-rate about it, except the toilettes of the ladies in the audience.

But whether a young lady prefers the constant society of a gentleman or gentlemen at her theatre-parties or in her walks, her rides, her drives, or her church-going, the point that makes her life in America different from any European experience is that she is free as the air to dispose of herself as she thinks best. It can scarcely be said that any part of the mode of life described above is likely to contribute much towards making people wiser, and a disposition towards mere enjoyment is apt to be much contemned by superior people who are impressed with the many difficult problems in life which have to be solved, and in the solution of which they themselves may be aiding. But it must be remembered how few of us are superior, or have any intention—even granting we have the ability—to apply our leisure time to schemes for the improvement of ourselves or of our fellow-creatures; and if we don't get the amusement to which we, rightly or wrongly, think ourselves entitled in one way, we will attempt it in another. Pretty constant social intercourse is good for the great mass of young people, even if a little frivolity be superinduced. But if ladies and gentlemen are to associate together, let their proper relative positions be maintained. Don't let us get and keep the wrong side uppermost.

And notwithstanding the luxury in which these young ladies are brought up, it is a common thing to see them marry men without a shilling of fortune except their brains, and after having been surfeited with every kind of attention and amusement, take up their quarters in a three-pair-back in "Bridal Row" without a murmur, and live for a season on about the cost of the bouquets sent to them in a previous season. As far as an outsider can judge, they make contented, loving, and faithful wives; and perhaps, after all, they cannot more worthily fulfil their destinies.

The records of the Sanitary Commission, too, during the war showed wonderful achievements on the part of American ladies, and of these New York claimed no small share; and the splendid charitable institutions of the city itself bear witness that these duties are in no way neglected.

It does not follow that work will not be well done because play is well done. And although the walks and the rides, the drives and the dinners, the croquet-parties and the evening parties, of ordinary young people may seem to be matters of very trivial interest or importance, it must be remembered that the sum of these small daily incidents powerfully affects the disposition, the manners, and the bearing of whole sections of society. We in England are too much tempted to think that because the best specimens of our own countrywomen and countrymen show types that are very rarely equalled and never excelled—so that the words English lady and English gentleman convey, and convey rightly, to our mind quite a distinct and different notion from mere "lady" or "gentleman"—therefore we are entitled to believe that our average

Briton holds something of a superior social rank to all foreigners. But when the choice specimens have been culled out, the fact is that, owing to our inequality of condition, the residuum in Great Britain is sometimes of a dull, pompous, selfish, ungenial nature, and may learn something even from much-maligned New York.

CONCLUSION:

WITH A FEW WORDS ON BIMETALLISM.

It is perhaps a work of supererogation to write a conclusion to so slender a bundle of materials, particularly as I have no definite conclusion to offer; for I hold entirely with the Frenchman that "si un livre porte un enseignement ça doit être malgré son auteur par la force même des faits qu'il raconte." But, unhappily, not one person out of a thousand ever really reads or masters facts and figures—especially figures. They are, generally speaking, regarded as a blot on creation, particularly from the literary man's point of view, although there are many tastes in literature. I once even heard of a gentleman who said that he "enjoyed reading Euclid, but found him too systematic!" He no doubt possessed a phenomenal *flaire* for the neglected nooks and by-ways of *belles-lettres,* and one cannot expect to have many readers of his peculiar taste. The lovers of the triangles are rare— of figures rarer. The moment we descry them in the distance we make up our minds to skip. But facts are facts. Let me therefore recapitulate the most important of them by way of summary.

For us in England the chief material considerations in viewing the New World are that, alongside of our little island teeming with population, we have moored (so to say) vast sparsely peopled continents, capable of producing all the food that our people require. We have lent them the money to build their railroads (which in some cases they do not repay); we have given them the greater part and the best part of their population; we have created a credit for their securities nearly equal to our own national credit—a credit which has sometimes been abused; we have built steamers to carry their products to our shores at marvellously low rates, and entry free, with the consequence that grain from Minnesota, California, Canada, or India, and beef and mutton from Australasia or Argentina, can be delivered in London at less cost of carriage than the same articles from Yorkshire forty years ago. This is a material revolution, and is at last beginning to make our farmers sit up and open their eyes. During these forty years we have, more and more, come to live and move and have our being by the New World. We have only to glance at the tables of our imports and exports to realise what we should have been without it. Meantime our population as a whole has never been so well off. It is true that in the last twenty years the small class of landowners and farmers has suffered, but not the masses of the people, agricultural or manufacturing, comparing their position with any former period. Their money wages are higher, and the purchasing power of these wages very much greater. But the New World has forced great changes on us. It is the key to the triumph of the Democracy. It is the key to the landowners' difficulty in Ireland, and goes some length towards explaining the demand for Home Rule. It is the key to the landowners' difficulty in England, and is now precipitating on us a radical reform of our system of land tenure. Would that the cure of these particular difficulties were as easy to arrive at as the key. The knowledge of the cause comes, but the wisdom enabling us to apply the remedy lingers.

Again, the New World is building for itself (has already built for itself, one may say) a wall against the products of our manufacture. That wall will, I think, be levelled some day; but it is difficult to be certain, when that time comes, that we shall get much aid or comfort from the levelling. The United States are our most formidable competitors in trade and commerce, and as time goes on and they perfect their processes, we may find that if they adopt free trade, in the long-run they may be able to undersell us in manufactured goods in neutral markets, and even in our own home markets. They have all our adaptability, they have all our elemental advantages in plentiful supplies of coal and iron, and *if* we join in fixing an international ratio for them between the value of silver and gold, they will have more than all our capital, and they will become the strongest banking power in the world: they have unrivalled water-force for the generation of electricity, and they have nothing else to do, nothing else to think of, except industrial production. The mental anxiety and worry for us in England of considering or fearing whether our next complication or war will be in Europe, Asia, or Africa, is a prodigious handicap in this commercial competition. Never for a day have we our minds quite free from this dread; and the risk cannot be expressed exactly in figures —in a rate of insurance, for instance,—it is "a spirit diffused through time and space," impalpable—but, as some one has said, " It is the impalpable that has prevailing weight." In other words — It is fate. " Our days are heritors of days gone by:" and all that we can practically do to help ourselves is, where possible, to curtail our responsibilities, and, particularly, to be careful of entering with a light heart into fresh responsibilities. Sooner or later they will come back on us.

Another practical thing we can do is to raise the question whether it is permissible for our own colonies to tax our manufacturers.

It is taxation without representation on our part. The boot is on the other leg now. With foreign nations we cannot help ourselves—we have no *locus standi*. But if our colonies (which are held as a part of ourselves) are allowed to treat us as foreigners, their benefit to us *as colonies* is problematical. We throw the ægis of protection over them, and in return they mulct us in duties for their trade protection. It is a one-sided arrangement. Is not the principle of *do ut des* practicable? Whatever import duties they may see fit to levy on the goods of foreign nations, our colonies ought to open their ports freely to our manufacturers as we open our ports to their products. In this way we would receive a *quid pro quo* which would relieve *pro tanto* our handicap in competition with the United States.

One of the objects of this little volume (very inadequately compassed, I am afraid) is to endeavour to discriminate between the sentimental view and that which I hold to be the true sentiment in regard to the New World. It is a sentimental view, and, in my belief, an historically untrue view, to look on the New

World as merely an expansion of England—or that Canada and Australia are, as a matter of fact, a part of England as Yorkshire is a part of England. Although many of their leaders may not acknowledge it, although they may passionately protest against it, onlookers are aware that it is undeniable that these two colonies take their tone of political thinking and acting more from America than from England. And American notions are not wholly English; they are crossed with many other strains. For instance, we must never forget that although France lost the material occupancy of the New World, she nevertheless left there the indelible impress of revolutionary ideas—and the force of the ideas has perhaps been really greater and more enduring, in some ways, than the force of the later occupancy. We must always bear this in mind in our dealings with the New World. Its ways are not exactly our ways, nor its purposes and ideals our purposes and ideals.

Meantime we have free trade all to ourselves, and we get our food cheap and plentiful; and the practical moral I draw from the present state of things agricultural in this country is, that it would have been very useful to our farmers and landowners, and would have saved them much loss, if they had taken the trouble to make themselves more intimately acquainted —if they had kept themselves more thoroughly *au courant* (up to date, as the phrase goes) —with the extraordinary rapid progress the New World has been making in the development of railways in the last five-and-twenty years. The results were clearly predicable. We must shoot the folly as it flies.

Now we must turn our attention to silver, which is going to be the next most important and burning question. And here, again, the New World has the *beau rôle*. There are States in America, like Nevada, Colorado, and New Mexico, which contain almost incredible masses of unmined silver. At Washington the treasury vaults bulge out with silver, coined and uncoined, continually requiring fresh accommodation to be built for it. The whole country is covered with silver certificates. Silver is the present dreadful difficulty and danger to American finance. Unless she gets the rest of the world's help, she must break under the load—break, in banking parlance.

That is, she will be unable to continue on a gold basis. Four years ago I drew attention to this danger (see pp. 258, 259). It is in the mouths of all men who know America. It won't break her productive power, though a great currency crisis may temporarily cripple it. And her currency is in an almost inextricable muddle. Naturally, in her trouble, she turns to sympathetic neighbours. We all do so in trouble. She wishes the rest of the world to pull the chestnuts out of the fire. We are going to send representatives to the Bimetallic Conference, but we must keep our weather-eye open to see who is going to get the advantage from any international arrangement that may be proposed for fixing a ratio between the value of silver and gold. The Americans are a very smart people, and we must take care that we get as much as we give in our dealings with them, otherwise we may find, after a time, that they have all the gold and we have— the experience and their silver. We may have a very soft, and even a sentimental, side to the New World, but really we must draw the line somewhere in placing ourselves at its feet. Business is business; and I fail to see at the present juncture why we should aid in giving this tremendous bonus to American property. Any critic who may have taken the trouble to read this volume will no doubt refer me to p. 235, where, fifteen years ago, I said a very few words on the subject. Bimetallism was then being taken up by the new school of political economy, and all of us who were in business were very anxious to find some panacea—some easement —for the throes of currency contraction produced all over the world by Germany's demonetisation of silver. None of us, I think, then realised the possibilities of the increased production of silver by improved machinery, and the increased facilities of carriage by railroads from the Far West. It seemed then that something had to be done for our Indian trade, and that our gain in that direction would compensate the risk of a general depreciation of currency. But what has happened in these fifteen years? *The fall in the prices of commodities has taken place.* The deed is done. Low prices are not in themselves objectionable. It is *instability* in prices that murders legitimate commerce. A "boom" is really worse, because more dangerous, than a gradual subsidence in prices. Both ought to be avoided if possible. But any great and sudden changes in nominal values convert whole peoples into masses of gamblers. Nothing can be more demoralising. Fifteen years ago America was just recovering from a long period of profound commercial depression. Her financial position was very safe, and her currency comparatively sound. Even then the mixture of gold, silver, and paper left much to be desired, and it was perhaps foolish not to have foreseen the magnitude of the proposal for helping to fix an international ratio *at that time*. But circumstances have meanwhile completely changed. Nobody could then have foreseen—or at any rate it required a great deal of seeing to foresee—that America would have become so loaded up with silver as is the case to-day.

Now it is painfully plain—it scarcely requires to be pointed out—that she is reeling under the insupportable weight; and why our poor "army of the orderly annuitants" —as George Meredith calls the holders of consols, debenture stocks, rent-charges, &c. —should be called upon to relieve the sturdy and prosperous Americans from their burden I fail to perceive, even if we admit and throw in the advantage to our Indian trade, and the making good of the pensions of our Indian civil servants. *Est modus in rebus.* No doubt this "army of the orderly annuitants" is fair food for the satirist and the socialist; but they are the prop and mainstay—the very life's blood—of the great Conservative party. There are comparatively few of them in the New World; and perhaps it is difficult to justify their existence now, when "the world in every part is pregnant with the new creed"; but it will be hard on them if their special defenders go back on them. For if the object aimed at is not a great appreciation of the price of commodities, or, in other words, a great depreciation—an incalculable future depreciation — of all fixed incomes, then what is it? I think we may leave our socialist friends to take care of that department. They are quite strong enough as it is. It is scarcely the time now for the leader of the Conservative party of the Commons in England (even speaking as a private member) to dangle Bimetallism before the eyes of an excited electorate before any kind of real scheme has been formulated, or any ratio fixed as possible or probable between silver and gold. The threat against property is often only thinly veiled. It reminds one of the word "ransom," used by another distinguished defender of law and order. It seems to me to be one of the most dangerous symptoms of the most dangerous disease of our time—I mean political poker-playing. Every one is going "a hundred better" over every one else all round the table. Bluffing is no doubt a very pretty game until some one calls your hand—and then? Well, then, it is the end of you. We, who are in touch with the city, have no reason to fear Bimetallism, as far as our own pockets are concerned. We shall be among the first to know when it is coming; and then for the steady-going people it will be a mere question of selling property with fixed incomes, and buying any real property, such as good ordinary stocks; but for the speculators the cry will not be "put money in thy purse," but " put margins in thy pocket, and buy with borrowed money anything and everything"; and the cheapest stocks will be the most profitable, for they must all go up as the silver counters are thrown into the pool. It will be the biggest " boom " of our time, or of any time—an unparalleled measure of inflation. But it will be hard on large classes, particularly on the widows and orphans of people of large property and of small property—the people who cannot turn quickly round and " bull" stocks—whose funds are for the most part tied up in trusts. It will be hard on the wage-earners, for their wages will not advance so quickly as the price of commodities will rise. It will be hard on all salaried people— on poor clerks in the city, and poorer clerks in holy orders; on judges and civil servants, on solicitors, barristers, and struggling doctors, whose fees are fixed by long custom ; on the greater part of the knights and dames of the Primrose League, who are mostly numbered among the idle rich, and form the rank and file of the "army of orderly annuitants." And the unkindest part of it all is that the blow is threatened by Mr Balfour, whom they have all hitherto called "the blessed." On the other hand, Bimetallism will be a gain to the landowners, it will be a gain to the farmers—and they have no doubt had a hard time the last twenty years, but they took the cream of things before that, and the railways made their money for them without much effort on their own part—and it will be a most inestimable boon to the stock-gamblers. They are always ready to sell their souls for "a boom"—for anything that will cause fluctuations in prices.

From the point of view of good Radicals and Socialists there would be, I fancy, little predisposition against any reasonable scheme that would really *benefit* the "have-nots" at the expense of the "haves." But I do not think it goes quite the length of taking measures to sacrifice the interests of the propertied class in England in order to help the Americans, who are so exceedingly well able to take care of themselves. They may play any pranks they like with their currency in the United States—and they have been playing extraordinary pranks in the last fifteen years. They will have their crisis, and in a few years' time it will pass away without much serious harm being done, for they have their wide country behind them. By it they must prosper, do what they will —almost in spite of themselves. Their prosperity does not really hang on the slender thread of credit. New York is not yet the banking centre of the world.

But before Bimetallism becomes a question of practical politics in England, I would venture to point out that, after the events of 1890 in the city of London, we have to be extremely careful not to injure further our national financial credit in the estimation of foreign nations: and it is difficult quite to realise (unless one lives a good deal abroad) what a shattering shock was dealt to us at that time. Other nations do not love us: they are naturally jealous; and financial credit is the most delicate of all growths—sensitive as the sensitive plant. A speech from the leader of the Conservative party in England in favour of Bimetallism will certainly set people thinking and talking in every business city from San Francisco to St Petersburg. Cæsar's wife must be above suspicion; and we must never—we can never—for one moment forget that we in England—being the banking centre of the world—live on, and are dependent on, our credit as no other nation in the world is, or ever has been. We know what a pound sterling is to-day. We know not what it may become if we attempt to play the fool with it. On that day it will indeed be difficult to say what it is or what it may become. And we have no great West behind us. The breaking of the small wheel of credit would be to us an irreparable break.

Let us then relegate Bimetallism to the region alone fitted for its discussion—namely, in pamphlets, magazine articles, or debating clubs. The subject does not lend itself to discussion in political meetings. It is like metaphysics. Nobody really knows anything about either subject, and it pleases us all to have something to talk about or write about—all in a circle, where one can never lay hold of the end of anything, and at the end nobody is a penny the better nor a penny the worse. But a juggle with the currency is a very awkward question to chuck into the arena of the political and party scuffle.

And if the Conservative party are going to adopt Bimetallism as a plank in their platform, together with other revolutionary fads, and if they come into power again and can carry them through the two Houses, let us hope, at any rate, that provision may be made for referring such measures specifically to the general electorate, before they become law, by means of a *referendum ad hoc*. The consequences of these revolutionary measures will be more far-reaching by a long way than the consequences of granting a measure of Home Rule to Ireland, and we ought to have the *referendum* as a final check on all these great changes. There is nothing like the " sober second thought." We have not the constitutional guards that the United States possess to prevent too hasty action on the part of temporary majorities, as has been so often pointed out to us of late years, and by none more forcibly than by the late Sir Henry S. Maine. We all know that there is no logical halting-place between the ascertained right of the majority and the Divine Right; and the Divine Right is no longer appealed to in the political sphere. No doubt the "tendency of the time" is to create the Commonwealth into "a mortal god,"—as Hobbes called it long ago. But even a mortal god is all the better of checks on hasty action. We ought to pray for more "lucidity of thought" to be granted to our leaders, whether Radical or Conservative. Whoever is going to steer our barque—this realm of England—in the near future through the rough seas of our "wild, windy modern time," will require a great deal of lucidity. "The deep moans round with many voices." Let us not be left, when the old pilot is no longer at the helm—

> "Nave senza nocchiero in gran tempesta
> Non donna di provincie, ma—casino."[1]

Let us not be turned into a great gambling-machine by inoculating our currency with unlimited silver.

I am afraid that my gentle reader will think that this little infant takes "a most unconscionable time in dying"; but I have now really come to my conclusion, which is to ask any one who may be kind enough to

[1] Purg. vi. 77.

peruse these pages through, to remember that the earliest dated papers were written some twenty years ago, when there were no board schools, when comparatively few people interested themselves in the material welfare of our agricultural labourers (they had no votes in those days), when it was highly unpopular to advocate "the re-marrying the people to the land," when the dogmas of the old political economy were still held to be binding in their fullest force, when any praise or even appreciation of America and things American was frigidly cold-shouldered in English society, when the girls in England were still rather " a down-trodden nationality." All these things are changed now. From unpopular causes they have become fashionable fads, and the pendulum has, naturally enough, swung back far to the other side—too far, perhaps. It is well that justice should be done; but more than justice is injustice. I merely mention this to explain a certain bias in my own writing during these twenty years —there is an amount of " work on the ball" (if I may use an illustration from cricket) which would be quite unnecessary and out of place to-day. The times are changed, and we are changed with them. I conclude with Bacon: "It may be in civil states a Republic is a better policy than a kingdom. Yet God forbid that lawful kingdoms should be tied to innovate and make alterations."

THE END.

www.ingramcontent.com/pod-product-compliance
Lightning Source LLC
Chambersburg PA
CBHW030736230426
43667CB00007B/731